Culture and Psyche

The essays in *Culture and Psyche* map the Indian psyche—its various facets affected by the culture that is so distinct from the culture of the Western world.

Sudhir Kakar is a psychoanalyst, novelist, and a well-known scholar in the fields of cultural psychology and the psychology of religion and has also taught at several universities in India, the United States, and Europe. Currently, he is Adjunct Professor of Leadership at INSEAD, France and lives in Goa. His many honours include the Kardiner Award of Columbia University, Boyer Prize for Psychological Anthropology of the American Anthropological Association, Germany's Goethe Medal, Distinguished Service Award of Indo-American Psychiatric Association, and fellowships of the Institutes of Advanced Study in Princeton and Berlin as also the Bhabha, Nehru, and ICSSR National fellowships. His sixteen books of non-fiction and four of fiction have been widely translated around the world.

GW00599482

Also by Sudhir Kakar

The Inner World

Kamasutra
(edited and translated by, with Wendy Doniger)

The Essential Writings of Sudhir Kakar

Tales of Love, Sex and Danger

Shamans, Mystics and Doctors

Identity and Adulthood
(edited volume)

The Indian Psyche

Indian Childhood

Culture and Psyche
Selected Essays

SECOND EDITION

SUDHIR KAKAR

OXFORD
UNIVERSITY PRESS

OXFORD
UNIVERSITY PRESS

YMCA Library Building, Jai Singh Road, New Delhi 110001

Oxford University Press is a department of the University of Oxford.
It furthers the University's objective of excellence in research, scholarship, and
education by publishing worldwide in

Oxford   New York
Auckland   Cape Town   Dar es Salaam   Hong Kong   Karachi
Kuala Lumpur   Madrid   Melbourne   Mexico City   Nairobi
New Delhi   Shanghai   Taipei   Toronto

With offices in
Argentina   Austria   Brazil   Chile   Czech Republic   France   Greece
Guatemala   Hungary   Italy   Japan   Poland   Portugal   Singapore
South Korea   Switzerland   Thailand   Turkey   Ukraine   Vietnam

Oxford is a registered trade mark of Oxford University Press
in the UK and in certain other countries

Published in India
by Oxford University Press, New Delhi

ISBN-13: 978-0-19-569668-4
ISBN-10: 0-19-569668-9

Typeset by Guru Typograph Technology, New Delhi 110 075
Printed in India by Roopak Printers, Delhi 110 032
Published by Oxford University Press
YMCA Library Building, Jai Singh Road, New Delhi 110 001

Contents

Contents

Preface to the Second Edition

I have made some additions and subtractions to this edition, the former more than the latter. What has been added are three new essays, 'Culture and Psychoanalysis: A Personal Journey', 'Rumours and Riots', and 'On the Psychology of Islamist Terrorism'. These essays are related to the overall theme of this book, and were published after the first edition of this book came out. What has been subtracted is the essay 'Modernity and Female Childhood', which is available in a considerably expanded version in a recent book *The Indians: Portrait of a People*. The first chapter has been shortened and is now titled 'Introduction: Culture in Psychoanalytic Thought'.

As for some repetitions, unavoidable in a collection of essays published in diverse journals, I can only ask for the reader's indulgence.

Goa   SUDHIR KAKAR
December 2007

Preface to the First Edition

Collecting and ordering what is scattered—memories, parts of life and self—is pre-eminently a middle-aged activity, a tribute we pay to intimations of our mortality. It may well be this simple yet powerful urge which propelled the collection of these writings in book form. Most of the papers—some slightly edited for the book—have been published earlier in different psychoanalytical journals. The previously unpublished essays—'Culture in Psychoanalysis', intended to give an introductory perspective, and 'Modernity and Female Childhood', which aims to provide a better gender balance to the collection—were written in 1994–95, during my stay at the Institute of Advanced Study, Berlin.

Even in their scattering, there is nevertheless a unity of intent and method in these essays. As far as purpose is concerned, most of the essays essentially strive for a psychoanalytic understanding of aspects of culture in India and, reflexively, the light this understanding can throw back on the tenets and models of psychoanalysis itself. In other words, my psychoanalytic listening to cultural voices is not a unidirectional activity but is guided by an interactive and intersubjective approach. As for the implicit method, most essays combine, to varying extents: one, the socio-cultural context of a specific problem; two, the hypotheses generated from clinical work with Indian patients on the way the culture has shaped the collective subjectivity in relation to this problem; and three, going back to the culture to test these hypotheses through an examination of collective fantasy, i.e. looking for the confirming presence (or absence) of the particular subjectivity—hypothesized from clinical work—in various products of the cultural imagination.

Except for the the two case histories, these essays are of comparatively recent origin. Written during the last seven years, they may be said to belong to the discipline of cultural psychology, with the culture in this case being Indian and the psychology of the psychoanalytic kind. Although I used the term many years ago (Kakar, 1982), defining it tersely as the 'interplay between the individual and his culture' (p. 7), it is only in the last decade that cultural psychology, with its non-Platonic interpretive stance, has become a vibrant and exciting new field, rapidly differentiating itself from the related fields of cross-cultural psychology, ethnopsychology and psychological anthropology (Shweder, 1991). From my own psychoanalytical viewpoint, cultural psychology is the study of that part of an individual's representational world which is shaped by his/her membership of a particular cultural group and which can be brought into sharper focus by comparing it with the representational worlds of individuals belonging to other cultures. I hope these essays make a small contribution to this new discipline.

REFERENCES

Kakar, S. (1982), *Shamans, Mystics and Doctors*, New York: Knopf.
Shweder, R. (1991), *Thinking Through Cultures*, Cambridge, Mass.: Harvard Univ. Press.

1

Introduction: Culture in Psychoanalytic Thought

It is now rarely disputed that the broader intellectual currents of a time, its Zeitgeist, have a profound influence on the way problems in the human sciences are formulated and systems of knowledge elaborated. The impact of nineteenth-century European intellectual, scientific, and moral concerns of Freud's thought, for instance, is sufficiently well-documented without in any way undermining his claim to genius. I believe it would be a fascinating exercise to link the various changes in psychoanalysis over the last one hundred years with the vicissitudes of Western intellectual and social history in the twentieth century. The developments in classical theory, such as ego psychology in the United States, the birth of other models which underplay if not explicitly deny the classical drive theory today and Freud's structural model in favour of an emphasis on 'object relations', Lacan's gloss on Freud and Kohur's 'self-psychology'—all would feature in the study. That such an effort must be confined to what is generally called the 'West', is due to the nature of the psychoanalytic enterprise which continues to derive its intellectual sustenance and creative impulse from European, North American, and increasingly Latin American centres without, as yet, any significant contributions from the non-Western civilizations.

From our vantage point at the beginning of the twenty-first century, we have little difficulty in discerning the impact of one of the more influential intellectual currents of our time—post-modernism—on contemporary psychoanalytic theories and practice. Although post-modernism consists of many stands, it has some common postulates which demand a response and serious engagements from all human sciences, including psychoanalysis. The core of post-modernism, as I understand it, would consist of the following statements: All social knowledge is relative in the sense that it is inextricable from its cultural and historical contexts and, especially, from its embeddedness in the power relations of a society; knowledge is not 'out there' to be discovered but is created or (to use a fashionable post-modernist term) 'socially constructed'; knowledge systems are not in the possession of some 'truth' but can only be evaluated on the basis of their aesthetic criteria such as plausibility, coherence—'attractiveness' in general—or the pragmatic criterion of their 'usefulness' for the needs of a particular culture at a particular time (Leary, 1994).

Besides encouraging a subjectivist, social-constructionist view of psychoanalysis (Atwood and Stolrow, 1984; Hofman, 1992) and empha-sizing its nature as a 'narrative' enterprise (Spence, 1982), the irreverent streak in post-modernism has also had a salutary effect on psychoanalytic writing which in its rightful pursuit of seriousness sometimes tends to get ponderously exegetical and given to making solemn ex-cathedra pro-nouncements. The post-modern intellectual surround, in which con-temporary analysts operate, has encouraged them to discuss observations and experiences from analytic practice—to 'tell it the way it is'—even when these undermine some of the cherished constructs of older theories and classical analytical technique. In fact, the creativity of contemporary psychoanalysis, even when its demise as a clinical discipline is repeatedly proclaimed, is in many ways reminiscent of its founding years when a spate of original and innovative papers were being published by Freud and his brilliant, sometimes quirky, disciples.

Whereas psychoanalytic creativity in the early years of the discipline was more centripetal, contributing to the construction of a single, grand enterprise, the contemporary creativity is more centrifugal. Today, with a profusion of suggested models and theories 'no one can claim to occupy an Archimedian point from which all theories can be objectively studied and a judgment rendered as to which is the correct theory' (Phillips, 1991, p. 408). What is important in contemporary psychoanalysis, however, is that it has recaptured the essentially iconoclastic spirit of the discipline's fledgling years, even though its iconoclasm is now more often directed at its own gods of an earlier era. To give only one example, some contemporary analysts are redefining the nature of analytic interaction, stressing the inescapable subjectivity of the analyst in the analytical situation and suggesting that he or she can never know the 'truth' about the internal state of a patient but only about his own. In France, the birthplace of some of the major constituent post-modern thoughts, many analysts believe that interpretations should be considered more as stimuli to the patient's self-investigation than as 'truths' about his or her mental life. In a recent paper,

Owen Renik (1993) not only questions the very notion of the traditional ideal of the dispassionate, objective analyst, but even contests the desirability of such a figure. He believes it pointless to ask an analyst to set aside his personal values and views of reality, his assumptions and psychological idiosyncrasies while he engages in the analytical activity of listening to the patient and interpreting the communications from the couch. All the analyst can do is become aware of the way his or her subjectivity influences analytic work and that, too, not in any prophylactic manner but only *after* the fact. To believe that the analyst can minimize his personal involvement in clinical work is to be falsely complacent and hold on to a dangerous illusion. There is no ideal analyst—neither Freud's 'reflecting mirror' listening to his patients with 'free floating attention', nor Bion's listener 'without memory, feelings, or desire'. Irrevocably entangled in his subjectivity, no analyst has total 'empathy' or is an ideal 'container'.

Although the social-constructionist view of analytic interaction, and the role of the analyst as a participant observer with irreducible subjectivity have been subjects of recent discussion in psychoanalysis, another important item on the post-modern agenda, the cultural and historical relativity of all (including psychoanalytic) knowledge, continues to be neglected. There is still insufficient appreciation of the fact that in the intellectual climate of our times, the cultural and historical transcendence of psychoanalytic theories can no longer be taken for granted but has to be rigorously demonstrated. This is not due to any obdurate refusal by contemporary analysts to question the essentialist 'psychic unity of mankind' view underlying Freud's grand metapsychological constructions; it has more to do with the fact that with rare exceptions (Doi, 1973), non-Western contributions which could help in revising any European ethnocentrism in psychoanalysis have been virtually non-existent in the evolution of psychoanalytic discourse. In the various phases of its encounter with anthropology, which could conceivably have tempered its Western-cultural orientation, psychoanalysis has usually been in the privileged position in the sense that its relationship with anthropology has been asymmetrical; there has been psychoanalytical anthropology but not an anthropological psychoanalysis. Analysts have continued to regard ethnographic facts and the methods used to uncover them as belonging to the 'surface' of human behaviour and hence superficial; they are not considered 'deep' enough to merit the respectful attention given to the reports of practicing analysis. The few anthropologists among analysts—especially the pioneers of the psychoanalytic anthropology such as Geza Rohein and George Devereux—have reinforced the privileged position of psychoanalysis by applying psychoanalytic concepts to cultures, almost as if the former were a fixed set of tools, rather than a means of making analysts more culturally sensitive and reflective. According to Devereux (1978), for instance, any doubts about a universal, acultural conception of psychoanalysis were to be rigorously combated. For him, analysis was a science independent of all cultural thought models and any efforts to 'reculturalize' it were to be strongly resisted; a psychoanalysis with cultural connotations would no longer be a science but merely one of the myths of the occidental world. All that Devereux was willing to grant was the presence of an ethnic unconscious built from a specific constellation of defence mechanisms that a given culture brings to bear on human experience, and through which the necessary renunciation of universal wishes and fantasies can be achieved. Yet the cultural relativistic position of post-modern thought, coupled with social changes such as the sharp increase in multi-culturalism in many Western societies, have been resulting in more and more calls from analysts of varying persuasion in many different countries (Davidson, 1988; Yampey, 1989; Bergeret, 1993; Rendon, 1993) to re-examine the issue of culture in psychoanalysis and not shy away from any 'reculturalization', if found necessary.

Analysts have not always been fully aware of the extent to which modern Western cultural assumptions with regard to the fulfilled human life and human relationship continue to influence many normative psychoanalytic assertions diagnostic considerations. For instance, let us take the marriage relationship, always a vital component in the analysis of most adults. Although from today's vantage point (and thus from a different cultural viewpoint), most analysts would decry the phallo-centrism evident in Freud's discussion of martial conditions in his lecture on femininity (Freud, 1930), they would still be inclined to accept as 'natural' what are in fact Western cultural assumptions about marriage, namely marriage as an institution based on choice, self-selection, monogamy, and an intense, affective bond between the partners. Locked into a Western model which regards the husband–wife bond as the fulcrum of family organization, psychoanalysts have considered the capacity to establish a long-term intimacy with a partner of the opposite sex as a mark of emotional maturity, a sign of the 'genital character'. In societies with different principle of social and family organization—for example, the extended family where the primary bond is that of parent and son and, deriving from it, very high significance is accorded to the fraternal tie—one can conceive of case histories reporting progress in quite different terms, such as 'The patient's relationship with his brothers improved markedly and his sexual relationship with his mistress regained some of its earlier vitality. Increasingly, he began to think of taking a third wife to beget the some he did not have from his other wives so that the family line could be continued, to the great happiness of his elderly parents.'

Similarly, in terms of analytic practice, I do not believe that a European analyst can remain unaware of at least a kinesthetic tension, which in a particular session will influence his interaction with the Chinese patient who is speaking of the delights of eating a dog curried Tibetan-style or that a vegetarian Hindu analyst will not emotionally flinch when his European patient begins her session with an account of last night's consumption of a rare and bloody beef steak.

If cultural values and beliefs are a part of the irreducible subjectivity of the analyst, his or her individual psychology, it is logical to expect that given the Western dominance of psychoanalysis since its inception, it would be essentially modern Western cultural values and beliefs which permeate psychoanalytic theory and practice. Psychoanalysis itself can legitimately be regarded as a sub-culture of broader Western civilization, with a body of shared beliefs about the world and a number of social institutions, especially the family, and shared norms such as every child's right to parental love, empathy, and respect, the desirability of reflective awareness of one's inner states, and so on (Fancher, 1993). In other words, analysts too are locked into a specific cultural unconscious which consists of a more or less closed system of cultural representations that are not easily accessible to conscious awareness. Psychoanalysis, then, like any other therapy, is also—and cannot be anything else but—an enculturation. Moreover, I would suggest that within a broader psychoanalytic enculturation, we make our patients Freudian, Kleinian, Lacanian, etc., and then report on our constructions as if they already existed in these forms before our interventions and interpretations. For a discipline devoted to the pursuit of disillusionment in the best sense of the term, a discipline which believes that illusions should have no future, it is ironical that psychoanalysis has devoted so little effort to root out its own cultural illusions which continue to masquerade as 'natural' social and psychological facts.

Culture in Classical Psychoanalysis

Even though the space between 'creativity' and 'curiosity' in the indexes to most psychoanalytic journals and monographs is depressingly empty, there are some analysts who have paid attention to the issue of culture in psychoanalytic theory—Freud being, of course, the most notable.

Freud's concept of man was not as determinedly biologistic—as opposed to the social and cultural—as is commonly believed. In his introductory remarks to the psychology of groups (Freud, 1921), Freud had no hesitation in saying that in the individual's mental life someone else is invariably involved as a model, as an object, as helper, as an opponent—what we would today simply call the 'Other'—so that from the very beginning, individual psychology is at the same time social psychology as well. The relations of an individual to his parents, to his brothers and sisters, to the object of his love, to his physician—relationships which have been the chief subject of psychoanalytic research—are all social phenomena. Freud even warns against the very sin he is accused of committing—underestimating the influence of social customs that force women into passive situations (Freud, 1933) as compared to the role of any 'innate' factors in the psychology of women.

Freud was well aware of the influence exercised on the individual's personality by his membership of a stable cultural group which, following McDougall, he characterized as having a continuity of existence, self-consciousness, traditions and customs, interaction with other groups (perhaps in the form of rivalry), and a structure expressed in specialization and differentiation of the functions of its constituents. To the regret of many, Freud did not go on to discuss the role of the stable cultural group in individual mental life, choosing instead to elaborate on the emotional dynamics within temporary groups such as a crowd and artificial groups such as the church and the army.

In general, however, Freud's concern was not the impact of cultural differences on the evolution of mental life. His interest in culture (with a capital 'C' and used interchangeably with civilization) was in its mighty conflict with the primitive, the raw, and the instinctual—Culture's struggle against Nature—with the individual psyche as the battleground. Culture, in Freud's view, was an edifice built upon a foundation of coercion and renunciation of instincts and the question which engaged his attention in many of writings was 'whether and to what extent it is possible to lessen the burden of instinctual sacrifices imposed on man, to reconcile men to those which must necessarily remain and to provide a compensation for them' (Freud, 1927, p. 7).

In its global, undifferentiated aspect, culture certainly played an influential role in the development and functioning of the psyche, namely in the formation of the superego. In an oft-quoted passage Freud (1933) writes: 'The child's superego is in fact constructed on the model not of its parents but of its parents' superego; the contents which fill it are the same and it becomes the vehicle of tradition and of all the time-resisting judgements of value which have propagated themselves in this manner from generation to generation . . .'; he envisions the importance of cultural differences when he goes on to say, 'Mankind never lives entirely in the present. The past, the tradition of the race and of the people, lives on in the ideologies of the superego, and yields only slowly to the influences of the present and to new changes; and so long as it operates through the superego it plays a powerful part in human life, independently of economic conditions' (ibid., p. 66).

With the social upheavals in Europe during the late 1920s and 1930s in the aftermath of the First World War and the spread and influence of Marxist thought, 'society' began to play an important role in the writings of analysts such as Wilhelm Reich, Erich Fromm, Karen Horney, Otto Fenichel, and later Franz Alexander. Freud's conceptions of the social environment was more in terms of cultural traditions, what he called the 'group minds' of race, class, creed, and nation which an individual shared in (Freud, 1921, p. 129); the 'leftist' analysts (Reich, Fromm) on the other hand, emphasized the social class aspects of the environment, especially the production relations of a society—Freud's 'economic' factor—in the development of personality, a society's mode of production bringing about a specific social character. In Fromm's posthumous writings, the individual's experience of the self is completely determined by social factors and he advances the concept of a 'social filter', consisting of the group's language, logic, and moral code which determines social consciousness; an individual's perceptions are only available to him if they have passed this filter (Fromm, 1990).

Perhaps one of the first analysts to elaborate upon the cultural relativity of mental life was Karen Horney, later branded a deviant, a 'neo-' rather than a 'post-' Freudian. In her original and stimulating paper 'Cultural and Psychological Implications of Neuroses' (Horney, 1937), she suggested that there are not only cultural variations in customs—and thus in the realm of individual superego—but also at the basic level of drives and feelings. In a radical critique of Freud, Horney said that he was mistaken in regarding instinctual drives or object relationships commonly seen in Western culture as biologically determined 'human nature'. The 'pregenital' stage or the Oedipus complex were not biologically given and thus unalterable, but were culturally variable. Horney, however, did not go so far as to embrace the extreme culturalist position where individual psychology is inseparable from its cultural base. In defining what is neurotic, Horney believed that a satisfactory answer needed both psychological and cultural tools. The first characteristic of neurosis, its dynamic centre, was fear and defence; the fears and defences of the individual would, however, become neurotic only when they deviated in quantity or quality from the fears and defences patterned in his or her culture. Similarly, with regard to the second characteristic of a neurosis, the presence of inner conflict, the conflicts became neurotic only if they were sharper and more accentuated than the common conflicts existing in the culture.

Within the Freudian mainstream, Otto Fenichel, the author of the standard and magisterial textbook on the theory of neuroses, was one of the first committed culturalist among the post-Freudians. Starting from Freud's notion of the cultural part of personality—the superego—which mirrors not only the demands of the individual's parents but also of his society, Fenichel (1945; 1954) proceeded to give a cultural inflection to both the remaining constituents of the tripartite model: the ego and the id. Since the ego also mediates between the organism and the environment, it was logical to presume that the ego must have a different cast in different cultural environments. Moreover, since the ego is to a large extent a composite of the individual's early identification with the parents, teachers, and so on, its nature would vary with the qualities—to some extent cultural—of these models of identification.

As far as the id was concerned, Fenichel suggested that social institutions influenced the instinctual structure of people living under them through temptations and frustrations, through shaping desires and antipathies. He believed it was a misunderstanding of Freud's concept of instinct, which in its original German, *Trieb*, did not have the connotations of unchangeability or rigidity that has led people to regard Freud as a biological determinist. The essence of the psychoanalytic method and of Freud's writings is to demonstrate how instinctual attitudes, objects, and aims are changed under the influence of experience.

Culture in Ego Psychology

Heinz Hartmann, the great theoretician of ego psychology which is the pre-eminent post-Freudian school in the United States, also took up the issue of the role of culture in psychoanalysis in his essay 'Psychoanalysis and Sociology' (1944). There were certain instinctual tendencies and psychological developmental facts, such as the dependency and helplessness of the child, which are common to all human beings regardless of their culture. Cultures differed in the way they dealt with these facts and for Hartmann the question to be asked was, 'In what manner and to what degree does a given social structure bring to the surface, provoke or re-inforce certain instinctual tendencies or certain sublimations, for instance?' Culture influences personality in a variety of ways. There are the more superficial influences which do not reach the core mental structure but shape the choice of a person's rationalizations, the conceptual language he uses, as well as certain mental contents. Other cultural influences reach the core structure where they co-determine the degree of severity of the superego, the degree of the mobility of the ego, and the person's style of conflict resolution. Cultures also have an effect on the frequency and type of neuroses in a given society as well as on their symptomatology and the meaning a neurosis may have for a certain cultural group. Obsessive-com-pulsive symptoms of constant washing and cleanliness, for instance, may well be regarded as an expression of piety in a particular religious group. Moreover, since the kind of neuroses in Western civilization have chang-ed—from the hysterical disorders of Freud's time to the more prevalent narcissistic and character of disorders of today, cultural conditions also seem to modify the deep structure of personality though Hartmann did not elaborate on this process.

Perhaps the most radical thinker on the issue of culture in the post-Freudian tradition was Erik Erikson. He not only sought to bring the individual's cultural environment into the centre of theoretical discus-sion, but was also the foremost proponent of cultural relativism among the psychoanalysts. Strongly influenced in his thinking by his field trips to the Yurok and Sioux Indians in the 1940s, in the company of two an-thropologists, H. Scudder Mekeel and Alfred Kroeber, Erikson saw the relationship between culture and self in terms of an adaptive fit, the creation of a communal identity being indispensable to individual identity. Every culture, no matter how 'primitive', must strive for a 'strong ego' in a majority of its members in order that the individual emerges from a long and fearful infancy with a sense of identity and an idea of integrity. The individual's ego-identity is adapted to his community's particular habitat, its worldview, and its design for living which, among others, inculcates efficiency in its ways of technology and protects individual members against anxiety. Cultures do this work of adaptation primarily by giving specific meaning to early bodily and interpersonal experiences—what Erikson (1952) called 'organ modes and social modalities'—a language very different from traditional psychoanalytic descriptions in terms of the structural model. For example, a child who has just found himself able to walk, incorporates his culture's particular version of 'one who can walk' into his ego, be it 'one who will go far', 'one who will be able to stand on his own feet', 'one who will be upright', or 'one who must be watched because he might go too far' (Erikson, 1952, p. 207).

Erikson was psychoanalyst enough not to idealize cultures and their 'designs for living', or to believe that the fit between culture and individual was always perfect. Each culture created character types marked by its own mixture of defect and excess, and each culture developed rigidities and illusions, thus protecting the individual against the insight that no ideal, safe, and permanent state can emerge from the blueprint the culture has evolved. There were also limits to the cultural creation of the individual self. A culture could exploit somatic patterns (such as differences of sex and age) only within limits which assured health and vitality to most of its members; it could make demands on personal adaptation but only within limits which guard a manageable degree of anxiety and conflict; and it could dictate social roles only up to the point where a sense of community can make up for sacrifices in individual autonomy (Erikson, 1987).

Most contemporary analysts in the classical Freudian tradition, I believe, would subscribe to the modified essentialism of Fenichel and Hartmann's conclusions. They would not agree with the extreme culturally relativist position that cultural conditions can by themselves account for intrapsychic constellations or even the behaviour of individuals in a given culture; nor would they share the post-modernist belief that there is no essential human nature at all. They would resist the notion of the person as a *tabula rasa* without 'innate' desires, wishes, and fantasies although they may differ about the basis of this innateness being biology, universal conditions of human infancy, or a combination of the two. They would see the individual as greatly modifiable but not infinitely so, with mental life as the end product of a complex interaction between the individual's culture, family milieu, and his or her own needs and desire-based fantasies. In another, more dynamic formulation to which I would subscribe, the individual self is a system of reverberating representational worlds—representations of his culture, primary family relationships and bodily life—each enriching, constraining, and shaping the others as they jointly evolve through the life cycle (Ross, 1994).

Culture in Object-relations Schools

In different object-relations theories, most of which are indebted to the work of Melanie Klein, there is an extraordinary absence of the external world, and thus of culture. The discussions of theory and interpretations in analytical practice are almost always in terms of earliest childhood fantasies expressing instinctual tendencies—in Klein, especially those related to terrifying violence and orgiastic body functioning. Here, there are no real people with their cultural beliefs, values, customs, and traditions; interpretations are almost exclusively oriented towards a universal infantile fantasy life revealed in relation to the analyst—in the transference, leaving little or no room for the effect of cultural differences on mental life. For instance, the only reference to culture I could find in the writings of Melanie Klein is an account of her meeting with an anthropologist (Klein, 1977, p. 263) who disagrees with her presumption of a universal foundation for mental life. He tells Klein of a tribe where it is considered a weakness to show mercy to an adversary. On being asked whether there were no exceptions to this rule the anthropologist admits that there are three. First, if the enemy can place himself behind a woman so that up to a point he is covered by her skirt; second, if he can get into a man's tent; and third, if he can reach the safety of a sanctuary. Klein interprets, to the satisfaction of the anthropologist, that the woman's skirt, the tent, and the sanctuary are symbols of the good mother protecting the family where a hated sibling is safe from murderous impulses and can find safety. Whatever distortions of character are accepted or even admired, she concludes, all cultures are linked through the primal good mother (and the frightening, 'bad' one—she might have also added).

When object-relations theorists talk of culture they do so in the sense of 'high culture'—embracing art, literature, and religion. Their interest is not in the cultural creation of individual mental life but in the individual's creation of culture. Culture is thus the individual's generation of psychic and interpersonal life (Guntrip, 1971). In the work of Winnicott, for instance, culture fills what he calls the 'potential space' of the individual, the area between the 'me' and the 'not-me', which is neither in the world of imagination nor outside in the world of shared reality. It is the space of individual creativity, where symbols are used and where the world is continually woven into the texture of imagination. It is the place where art, literature, music, and religion are encountered and depends for its existence on the richness of the developing child's experiences. Winnicott's interest in the influence of culture in our sense is therefore limited to the issue of whether cultures facilitate or retard the child's creative experiencing (Winnicott, 1965; 1974).

Culture and Self-psychology

In his earlier writings, Kohut (1971) recognized the effect of the child's cultural milieu on the 'drive-curbing and drive-channeling structures' of the basic fabric of his psyche (p. 188); however, he believed an engagement with culture lay outside the task of psychoanalysis proper. Such knowledge may be tactically useful in analysis by constituting an act of intellectual mastery which gives support to the patient's ego but essentially belongs to the non-analytic realm of *etiology* rather than to the *generic* domain of psychoanalysis. The genetic approach in analysis relates to the investigation of those subjective psychological experiences of the child which usher in a chronic change in the distribution and further development of 'endopsychic forces and structures' (p. 258). The etiologic approach, on the other hand, relates to the investigation of those objectively ascertainable factors which, in interaction with the child's psyche as it is constituted at a given moment, may—or may not—elicit the genetically decisive experience. In other words, it is not the objective, perhaps culturally determined or co-determined 'event' but the subjective experiencing of this event by the individual which is decisive for psychoanalytic work.

In Kohut's later writings (1977; 1985), there is a perceptible greater interest in the influence of cultural differences on the development of the self. Culture enters self-psychology through the questions: How does the social milieu provide stimuli or lack of stimuli? How does it nourish, under-nourish, or warp the self? In formulations very similar to Erikson's discussion of identity development in various socio-cultural contexts, Kohut suggests that there are a wide variety of parental responses to the child which are non-pathogenic and do not interfere with psychic development even when they do not actively promote it. Within limits, such as the ones crossed by the parents' grossly sexual or counter-aggressive responses to a growing child's oedipal manifestations, there is a whole spectrum of parental responses which can be said to lie within the realm of normalcy. In patriarchal societies, for example, the parental attitudes towards the oedipal boy foster, as a result of his experiences at this stage of his life, the development of psyche characterized by a firm superego and a set of strong masculine ideals. This is a personality type which may be specifically adapted to the tasks of a frontier society or at least to a society in which the values of a frontier society still hold sway. In societies where gender differentiation has lessened, different parental attitudes may produce girls whose ideals and firmness of superego correspond more to those normally found in boys growing up in patriarchal societies—girls who may be specifically adapted to the tasks of a non-expansive society (Kohut, 1977, pp. 231–2).

In modern Western societies, Kohut believes, the child's participation in his parents' play and leisure activities can never provide his nuclear self with the same nutrients as his emotional participation in their work life—something which was more common in traditional societies. In work, the parents' competence and their pride in the work situation ensue that their selves are profoundly engaged and the core of their psyches most accessible to the empathic observer. Further, whereas children were earlier over-stimulated by the emotional (including erotic) life of their parents, they are now often under-stimulated. Formerly (in Freud's time?), the child's eroticism aimed at gaining pleasure led to inner conflict because of parental prohibitions and oedipal rivalries. Today, many children seek erotic stimulation to relieve loneliness and fill an emotional void (Kohut, 1977, pp. 269–71).

Psychoanalytic Understanding of Cultures

Most psychoanalytic observations on the role of culture in the development of the self have the character of principles derived from the author's particular theoretical orientation; they are, in Kohut's terminology, experience-distant rather than experience-near formulations. In contrast to the psychological anthropologists (whose work is not a subject of this essay), analysts have rarely had the opportunity to elaborate upon and show the effectiveness of these principles in concrete cultural contexts that vary sharply from those of Western societies. When they have done so, they have usually worn the anthropologist's hat instead of sitting behind the clinician's couch. There are indeed a number of reports in psychoanalytic literature on the analysis of individuals from different cultures or from different cultures or from different sub-cultures within a particular Western society (e.g. Sachs, 1937; Muensterberger, 1951; Babcock and Caudill, 1958; Schachter and Butts, 1968; Ticho, 1971). Direct analytic observations of a non-Western culture through the analysis of a number of persons belonging to that culture have been rare (Parin, Morgenthaler, and Parin-Matthey, 1963; Roland, 1988). The relatively small number of cases, short duration of the therapies, their conduct in a language which is not the patient's mother tongue, and, sometimes, the lack of the analytic setting raises as many questions as these accounts seek to answer. For instance, in the work of Parin et al. on the Dogon in West Africa, regarded as a classic in the genre, psychoanalytic interviews in French, in a face-to-face setting, were conducted for a few months with thirteen persons who had no wish to be treated or healed and a good part of whose motivation to collaborate with the European analysts' enterprise was to talk (or be seen talking) with high status Whites and to *receive* money for each session. These accounts, whatever their value for psychological anthropology, lack the elaboration of imagination and subjectivity of people living within the particular culture. What is missing are the narratives of conflict, passion, and despair which give psychoanalysis its distinctive cast—and perhaps its very life. They raise doubts whether the writers have a sufficient intimacy with the particular non-Western culture to make *psychoanalytic* contributions to its understanding. Lacking the intimate cultural knowledge that makes a pre-conscious sense of many unspoken 'texts' of a communication contained in infections, intonations, gestures, and in the ways in which something is *not* said, these accounts, say, of the Dogon in Africa and of Indian in New York and Bombay, are flat and unidimensional. They resemble portraits of Third-World natives drawn by Western travel-writers, journalists, and novelists, images of people who talk the European language with the quaint engagingness but whose inner life is bland and certainly far less complex than that of the writers' middle-class English, French, or American friends.

Intimacy with one's subject is perhaps the most important vehicle for conveying the authority of a patience of writing. Western writings on Indian inner life, psychoanalytic, literary, or anthropological, may be without gross misrepresentations of fact but, with rare exceptions, they are often marked by a nuance here, a false note there, a missing beat here, which slowly mount up in a text to insidiously undermine its rhetorical authority. There is, of course, some arrogance in undertaking a psychoanalytic study of another culture on the basis of very limited analytic work. Such arrogance is perhaps necessary and has on occasion yielded rich dividends. As the psychological anthropologist Gananath Obeyesekere (1990) notes in case of anthropology, one cannot study another culture without such arrogance for 'it defies ordinary common sense that a young person with imperfect language skills could go into the field and study another culture to present the native's point of view during the period of a year or, at the most, two' (p. 218).

One must not forget that the roots of this arrogance (self-confidence?) also lie in the historical structure of international power relations in the last two centuries between the Western and non-Western worlds. Although many persons in former Western colonies possess a deep and extensive knowledge imbibed since early childhood, of the language, history, literature, and society of at least one Western country—most highly educated men and a women in the Third World are natural 'occidentalists'—they have generally lacked the cultural self-confidence to comment on the Western society they know so well.

Psychoanalytic knowledge of a culture does not coincide with its anthropological, historical, or philosophical counterparts although there may be some overlap between them. It is primarily the knowledge of the culture's imagination, of its fantasy as encoded in its symbolic products. Much of this knowledge is embedded in the universe of the patient's language, especially the language of childhood. The analyst's awareness of this universe is important even if the analysis is conducted in a language which is not the patient's mother tongue. To given an example, in Punjabi, among boys there are four different words used for the vagina. These words not only refer to the imagined sizes of the female genitalia but are associated with fantasy structures ranging from deflowering a young virgin to the threatening, 'large' vagina of an older woman. Similarly, the images associated with the words for a penis range from the vulnerability of the little boy's organ to the power of and majesty of the paternal phallus. The use of the English 'penis' and 'vagina' will lead an analyst without such a psychoanalytic knowledge of the patient's culture to miss out on the exact imagery and the full range of affect associated with the patient's experience.

Psychoanalysts can help patients from different cultures because of their focus on the universal aspects of the patients' experiences, and because of their common humanity. They cannot, however, advance psychoanalytic propositions about a culture on the basis of such work. What good clinical work can do is generate hypotheses about the role of culture in intra-psychic life. The further testing of these hypotheses from case histories is best done (i.e. it comes closest to psychoanalytic intention and enterprise) by testing them in the crucible of the culture's imagination—its myths, art, fiction, cinema, and so on—before a psychoanalytic understanding of another culture can be formulated.

REFERENCES

Atwood, G.E. and Storlow, R.D. (1984), *Structure of Subjectivity Explorations in Psychoanalytic Phenomenology*, Hillsdale, J.J.: Analytic Press.

Babcock, C. and Caudill, W. (1958), 'Personal and Cultural Factors in Treating a Nisei Man', in G. Seward ed., *Clinical Studies in Cultural Conflict*, New York: Ronal Press.

Bergerer, J. (1993), 'Psychanalyse er universalite interculturelle', *Revue Francaise de Psychanalyse*, 57:3, 809–40.

Davidson, L. (1988), 'Culture and Psychoanalysis', *Contemporary Psychoanalysis*, 24: 1, 74–91.

Doi, T. (1973), *The Anatomy of Dependence*, Tokyo: Kodansha.

Devereux, G. (1978), *Ethnopsychoanalysis*, Berkeley: University of California Press.

——— (1980), *Basic Problems of Ethnopsychiatry*, Chicago: University of Chicago Press.

Erikson, E.H. (1952), *Childhood and Society*, New York: Norton.

——— (1987), 'Environment and Virtues', in S. Schlein ed., *A Way of Looking at Things*, New York: Norton, 503–21.

Fancher, R.T. (1993), 'Psychoanalysis as Culture', *Issues in Psychoanalytic Psychology*, 15:2, 81–93.

Fenichel, O. (1945), *The Psychoanalytic Theory of Neuroses*, New York: Norton.

——— (1954), *The Collected Papers of Otto Fenichel*, New York: Norton.

Freud, S. (1921), 'Group Psychology and the Analysis of the Ego', *S.E.* 18.

——— (1927), 'The Future of an Illusion', *S.E.* 21.

——— (1930), 'New Introductory Lectures', *S.E.* 22.

Fromm, E. (1990), *Die Entdeckung des gesellschaftlichen Unbewusstern. Schriften aus dem Nachlass*, Weinheim u. Basel.

Hartmann, H. (1944), 'Psychoanalysis and Sociology', in *Essays on Ego Psychology*, New York: Norton.

Hofman, I.Z. (1992), 'Some Practical Implications of a Social-constructionist View of the Psychoanalytic Situation', *Psychoanal. Dialogues*, 2, 287–304.

Horney, K. (1937), 'Cultural and Psychological Implications of Neuroses', in *The Neurotic Personality of Our Time*, New York: Norton.

Klein, M. (1977), *Envy and Gratitude*, New York: Dell Publishing.

Kohut, H. (1971), *The Analysis of the Self*, New York: Int. University Press.

——— (1977), *The Restoration of the Self*, New York: Int. University Press.

——— (1985), *Self Psychology and the Humanities*, New York: Norton.

Lear, K. (1994), 'Psychoanalytic Problems and Postmodern "Solutions"', *Psychoanal. Q.*, 63, 433–65.

Muensterberger, W. (1951), 'Orality and Dependence: Characteristics of Southern Chinese', in *Psychoanalysis and the Social Sciences*, New York: Int. University Press.

Parin, P., Morgenthaler, F., and Parin-Matthey, G. (1963), *Die Weissen Denken Zuviel*, Zurich: Atlantis Verlag.

Phillips, J. (1991), 'Hermeneutics in Psychoanalysis: Review and Reconsideration', *Psychoanalysis and Contemporary Thought*, 14, 371–424.

Rendon, M. (1993), 'The Psychoanalysis of Ethnicity and the Ethnicity of Psychoanalysis', *American Journal of Psychoanalysis*, 53: 2, 109–22.

Renik, O. (1993), 'Analytic Interaction: Conceptualizing Technique in Light of the Analyst's Irreducible Subjectivity', *Psychoanalytic Quarterly*, 62: 4, 553–71.

Ross, J.M. (1994), *What Men Want*, Cambridge, Mass: Harvard Univ. Press.

Sachs, W. (1937), *Black Hamlet: The Mind of an African Negro Revealed by Psychoanalysis*, London: G. Bles.

Schachter, J.S. and Butts, H.F. (1968), 'Transference and Countertransference in Interracial Analyses', *Journal of American Psychoanalytic Association*, 16: 792–808.

Spence, D. (1982), *Narrative Truth and Historical Truth: Meaning and Interpretation in Psychoanalysis*, New York: Norton.

Ticho, G.R. (1971), 'Cultural Aspects of Transference and Countertransference', *Bulletin of the Menninger Clinic*, 35(5): 313–26.

Winnicott, D.W. (1965), *The Maturarational Process and the Facilitating Environment*, London: Hogarth Press.

_____ (1974), *Playing and Reality*, London: Penguin Books.

Yampey, N. (1989), 'Psicoanalysis de la cultura', *Revista de Psicoanalisis*, 46: 3, 303–16.

2

Culture and Psychoanalysis:
A Personal Journey

My interest in the role of culture in psychoanalysis and psychology did not begin as an abstract intellectual exercise but as a matter of vital personal import. Without my quite realizing it at the time, it commenced when I started on my journey as a psychoanalyst more than 30 years ago upon entering a five-day-a-week training session with a German analyst at the Sigmund-Freud-Institut in Frankfurt. At first, I registered the role of culture in my analysis as a series of niggling feelings of discomfort whose source remained incomprehensible for many months. Indeed, many years were to pass before I began to comprehend the cultural landscape of my mind in more than a rudimentary fashion.

I earned very little at the time and in spite of my frequent complaints on my poverty from the couch, I was disappointed when my analyst was prompt in presenting his bill at the end of the month and did not offer to reduce his fees. Without ever asking him directly, I let fall enough hints that he could be helpful in getting me a better paying job—for instance, as his assistant in the Institute where he held an important administrative and teaching position. I felt betrayed and rejected when no practical assistance was forthcoming.

I did not have any problems in coming to my sessions in time but was resentful that my analyst was equally punctual in ending a session after exactly fifty minutes, sometimes when I had just got going and felt his involvement in my story had been equal to my own.

After undergoing analysis for some months, I realized that my recurrent feelings of estrangement were not due to cultural differences in forms of politeness, manners of speech, attitudes towards time, or even differences in aesthetic sensibilities. (To me, at that time, Beethoven was just so much

Revised version of an essay first published in *Social Analysis*, 50: 2, 2006.

noise, while I doubt if my analyst even knew of the existence of Hindustani classical music, which so moved me.) The estrangement involved much deeper cultural layers of the self, which were an irreducible part of my subjectivity as, I suppose, they were a part of my analyst's. In other words, if during a session we sometimes suddenly became strangers to each other, it was because each of us found himself locked into a specific 'cultural identity' that was rarely conscious. In my case, this cultural identity was an 'Indian-ness' which I was to spend many years elucidating. (Kakar, 1978, 1982, 1987, 1989, 1994; Kakar and Kakar, 2006)

A culturally Indian-ness or Indian identity is not an abstract concept, a subject of intellectual debate for academics, but something that informs the activities and concerns of daily life for a vast number of Indians while at the same time it guides them through the journey of life. How to behave towards superiors and subordinates in organizations, the kinds of food conducive to health and vitality, the web of duties and obligations in the family—all these are as much influenced by the cultural part of the mind as are ideas concerning the proper relationship between the sexes, or one's relationship to the Divine. Of course, for the individual Indian, this civilizational heritage may be modified or overlaid by the specific cultures of one's family, caste, class, or ethnic group. Yet an underlying sense of Indian identity continues to persist, even into the third or fourth generation in the Indian diasporas around the world, and not only when they gather together for a Diwali celebration or to watch a Bollywood movie.

At first glance, the notion of a singular Indian-ness—of an Indian identity—may seem far-fetched: How can one generalize about a billion people—Hindus, Muslims, Sikhs, Christians, and Jains—who speak 14 major languages and are characterized by pronounced regional and linguistic identities? How can one postulate anything in common among a people divided not only by social class but also by India's signature system of caste, and with an ethnic diversity typical more of past empires than of modern nation-states? Yet as attested to by foreign travelers throughout the ages, there is a unity or at least a harmony in this diversity that is often ignored or unseen because our modern eyes are more attuned to discern divergence and variance than resemblance. Indian-ness, then, is about similarities rather than the *surface* dazzle of differences among the inhabitants of this vast sub-continent, similarities produced by an overarching Indic, pre-eminently Hindu civilization that constitutes the 'cultural gene pool' of India's peoples.

This civilization has remained in constant ferment through the processes of assimilation, transformation, reassertion, and re-creation that came in the wake of its encounters with other civilizations and cultural forces, such as those unleashed by the advent of Islam in medieval times and European colonialism in the more recent past. The contemporary buffeting of Indic civilization by a West-centric globalization is only the latest in a long line of invigorating cultural encounters that can be called 'clashes' only from the narrowest of perspectives. Indic civilization is thus the common patrimony of all Indians, irrespective of their faith

In a contentious polity, where various groups loudly clamour for recognition of their differences, the awareness of a common Indian-ness, the sense of 'unity within diversity', is generally absent. Like the Argentinian writer Jorg Luis Borges' remark on the absence of camels in Koran because they were not exotic enough to the Arab to merit attention, the camel of Indian-ness is invisible or taken for granted by most of us. Our family resemblance begins to stand out in sharp relief only when it is compared to the profiles of peoples of other major civilizations or cultural clusters. A man who is an Amritsari in Punjab, is a Punjabi in other parts of India and an Indian in Europe; the outer circle of his identity, his Indian-ness, is now salient for his self-definition as also for his recognition by others. This is why, in spite of persistent academic disapproval, people (including academics in their unguarded moments) continue to speak of 'the Indians', as they do of 'the Chinese', 'the Europeans', or 'the Americans', as a necessary and legitimate shortcut to a more complex reality.

What are some of the building blocks of this Indian-ness or Indian identity? Here I will mention only some of the key ones: an ideology of family relationships in particular and relationships in general that derives from the institution of the joint family, a profoundly hierarchical view of social relations influenced by the institution of caste, an image of the human body and bodily processes that is based on the medical system of Ayurveda, a cultural imagination teeming with shared myths and legends that underscore a 'romantic' vision of human life, and a relativistic, context-sensitive way of thinking (Kakar and Kakar, 2006). Here, I can only give you a flavour of what I mean. Let me talk of relationships.

To begin with the specific relationship, in the universe of teacher-healers, I had slotted my analyst into a place normally reserved for a personal guru. From the beginning of the training analysis, it seems, I had preconsciously envisioned our relationship in terms of a guru–disciple bond, a much more intimate affair than the contractual doctor–patient relationship governing my analyst's professional orientation. In *my* cultural model, he was the personification of the wise old sage benevolently directing a sincere and hardworking disciple who had abdicated the responsibility for his own welfare to the guru. My guru model also demanded that my analyst demonstrate his compassion, interest, warmth, and responsiveness much more openly than is usual or even possible in the psychoanalytic model guiding his therapeutic interventions. A handshake with a 'Guten Morgen, Herr Kakar' at the beginning of the session and a handshake with a 'Auf Wiedersehen, Herr Kakar' at the end of the session, even if accompanied by the beginnings of a smile, were not even starvation rations for someone who had adopted the analyst as his guru.

Our cultural orientations also attached varying importance to different family relationships. For instance, in my childhood, I had spent long periods of my young life in the extended families of my parents. Various uncles, aunts, and cousins had constituted a vital part of my growing up experience. To pay them desultory attention or to reduce them to parental figures in the analytic interpretations felt like a serious impoverishment of my inner world.

On a general level, I realized later, our diverging conceptions of the 'true' nature of human relationships were a consequence of a more fundamental divide in our cultural view of the person.

If each of us begins life as a mystic, awash in a feeling of pervasive unity in which there is no distance between things and ourselves, then the process of sorting out 'me' from 'not-me' is one of the primary tasks of our earliest years. This task involves the recognition—later taken for granted, at least in most of our waking hours and in a state of relative sanity—that I am separate from all that is not-I, that my 'Self' is not merged with but detached from the 'Other'.

The experience of separation has its origins in our beginnings, although its echoes continue to haunt us till the end of life, its reverberations agitating the mind, at times violently, during psychological or spiritual crises.

The Indian gloss on the dilemmas and pain of banishment from the original feeling of oneness, the exile from the universe, has been to emphasize a person's enduring connection to nature, the Divine, and all living beings. This unitary vision of soma and psyche, individual and community, and self and world is present in most forms of popular culture even today. From religious rites to folk festivals, there is a common negation of separation and a celebration of connection.

The high cultural value placed on connection is, of course, most evident in the individual's relationships with others. The yearning for relationships, for the confirming presence of loved ones, and the psychological oxygen

they provide is the dominant modality of social relations in India, especially within the extended family. Individuality and independence are not
values that are cherished. It is not uncommon for family members, who
often accompany a patient for a first psychotherapeutic interview, to complain about the patient's autonomy as one of the symptoms of his or her
disorder. Thus, the father and elder sister of a 28-year-old engineer who
had psychotic episodes described their understanding of his chief problem
as one of unnatural autonomy: 'He is very stubborn in pursuing what
he wants without taking our wishes into account. He thinks he knows
what is best for him and does not listen to us. He thinks his own life and
career are more important than the concerns of the rest of the family'
(Kakar, 1987: 446). The high value placed on connection does not mean
that Indians are incapable of functioning by themselves or that they do not
have a sense of their own agency. What it does imply is a greater need for
ongoing mentorship, guidance, and help from others in getting through
life and a greater vulnerability to feelings of helplessness when these ties
are strained.

The yearning for relationships, for the confirming presence of loved
ones, and the distress aroused by their unavailability in times of need are
more hidden in Western societies, in which the dominant value system of
the middle class prizes autonomy, privacy, and self-actualization, and
holds that individual independence and initiative are 'better' than mutual
dependence and community. Could it be that my analyst was like some
other Western psychoanalysts who I was reading at the time, who would
choose to interpret this as a 'weakness' in the Indian personality?

But whether a person's behaviour on the scale between fusion and isolation is nearer the pole of merger and fusion with others or the pole of
complete isolation depends, of course, on the culture's vision of a 'good
society' and 'individual merit'. In other words, the universal polarities of
individual versus relational, nearness versus distance in human relationships are prey to culturally moulded beliefs and expectations. To borrow
from Schopenhauer's imagery, human beings are like hedgehogs on a cold
night. They approach each other for warmth, get pricked by the quills of
the other, and move away until, feeling cold, they again come closer. This
to-and-fro movement keeps being repeated until an optimum position is
reached wherein the body temperature is above the freezing point yet the
pain inflicted by the quills—the nearness of the other—is still bearable.
Independent of the positions our individual life histories had moved us to
select on this continuum, in my Indian culture, in contrast to my analyst's

German *Kultur*, the optimum position entailed the acceptance of more pain in order to get greater warmth.

One could thus as easily do a reverse pathologizing by saying that if one thinks of Eros not in its narrow meaning of sex but in its wider connotation of a loving 'connectedness' (where the sexual embrace is only the most intimate of all connections), then the relational cast to the Indian mind makes Indians more 'erotic' than many other peoples of the world. The relational orientation, however, also easily slips into conformity and conventional behaviour, making many Indians psychologically old even when young. On the other hand, the Western individualistic orientation has a tendency towards self aggrandizement, 'the looking out for Number One', and the belief that the gratification of desires—most of them related to consumption—is the royal road to happiness. In a post-modern accentuation of 'fluid identities' and a transitional attitude towards relationships, of 'moving on', contemporary Western man (and the modern upper-class Indian) may well embody what the Jungians call *puer aeternus*—the eternal youth, ever in pursuit of *his* dreams, full of vitality, but nourishing only to himself while draining those around him.

Let me add that I am not advancing any simplified dichotomy between my analyst's Western cultural image of an individual, autonomous self and a relational, transpersonal self of my own Hindu culture. Both visions of human experience are present in all the major cultures though a particular culture may, over a length of time, highlight and emphasize one at the expense of the other. What the advent of Enlightenment in the West has pushed to the background for the last couple of hundred years is still the dominant value of Indian identity, namely that the greatest source of human strength lies in a harmonious integration with the family and the group. It asserts that belonging to a community is the fundamental need of man. Only if man truly belongs to such a community, naturally and unselfconsciously, can he enter the river of life and lead a full, creative, and spontaneous life.

In practice, of course—and this is what makes psychoanalytic psychotherapy in non-Western societies possible—the cultural orientations of patients coming for psychoanalytic therapy are not diametrically opposite to those of the analyst. Most of non-Western patients seen by analysts in North America and Europe are 'assimilated' to the dominant culture of their host country to varying degrees, the contest between their original and new cultures not yet decisively tilted in the favour of one or the other. Similarly, in non-Western countries, the clients for psychoanalytic therapy—like their analysts—are westernized to varying degrees. For instance, they tend to be more individualized in their experience of the self than the bulk of their more traditional countrymen.

The emphasis on connection is also reflected in the Indian image of the body, a core element in the development of the mind. For Ayurveda, one of the chief architects of the Indian image of the human body, the body is intimately connected with nature and the cosmos, and there is nothing in nature without relevance for medicine. The Indian body image, then, stresses an unremitting interchange taking place with the environment, simultaneously accompanied by a ceaseless change within the body. Moreover, in the Indian view, there is no essential difference between the body and the mind. The body is merely the gross form of matter (*sthulasharira*), just as the mind is a more subtle form of the same matter (*sukshmasharira*); both are different forms of the same body-mind matter—*sharira*.

It is not only the body but also the emotions that have come to be differently viewed due to the Indian emphasis on connection. As some cultural psychologists (Shweder and Bourne, 1984) have pointed out, emotions that have to do with other persons, such as sympathy, feelings of interpersonal communion, and shame, are primary while the more individualistic emotions, such as anger and guilt, are secondary. The Indian psyche has a harder time experiencing and expressing anger and guilt but is more comfortable than the Western individualistic psyche in dealing with feelings of sympathy and shame. If pride is overtly expressed, it is often directed to a collective, of which one is a member. Working very hard to win a promotion at work or admission to an elite educational institution is only secondarily connected to the individual need for achievement, which is the primary driving motivation in the West. The first conscious or pre-conscious thought in the Indian mind is 'How happy and proud my family will be!' This is why Indians tend to idealize their families and ancestral background, why there is such prevalence of family myths and of family pride, and why role models for the young are almost exclusively members of the family, very frequently a parent, rather than the movie stars, sporting heroes, or other public figures favoured by Western youth.

Let me repeat that I am not an adherent of a simplified dichotomy between a European cultural image of an individual, autonomous self, and a relational, transpersonal self of Indian society. These prototypical patterns do not exist in their pure form in any society. Psychotherapy with middle-class Western patients tells us that autonomy of the self is as precarious in reality as is the notion of an Indian self that is merged in the surroundings of its family and community. In a sense, both are fictions;

their influence on behaviour derives not from their actual occurrence but from their enshrinement as cultural ideals.

As I said, I only wish to give a flavour of the deeper layers of what I have called Indian identity. I could go on, as I have done at other places, to highlight other fundamental differences and their consequences, such as in the perception of what is masculine and what is feminine or the hierarchical vision of Indian eyes. But my time is short and I would like to get back to my personal journey and what happened in my own psychoanalysis. Was it destined to fail because we were both embedded in our cultural identities? What could my analyst have done? Did he need to acquire knowledge of my culture and, if so, what kind of knowledge? Would an anthropological, historical, or philosophical grounding in Hindu culture have made him understand me better? Or was it a *psychoanalytical* knowledge of my culture that would have been more helpful? Psychoanalytic knowledge of a culture is not equivalent to its anthropological knowledge, although there may be some overlap between the two. Psychoanalytic knowledge is primarily the knowledge of the culture's *imagination*, of its fantasy as encoded in its symbolic products—its myths and folktales, its popular art, literature, and cinema.

Besides asking about the kind of knowledge we also need to ask the question 'Which culture?' Would a psychoanalytic knowledge of Hindu culture have been sufficient in my case? Yes, I am a Hindu but also a Punjabi Khatri by birth. That is, my overarching Hindu culture has been mediated by my strong regional culture as a Punjabi and further by my Khatri caste. This Hindu Punjabi Khatri culture has been further modified by an agnostic father and a more traditional, believing mother, both of whom were also westernized to varying degrees. Is it not too much to expect any analyst to acquire this kind of prior cultural knowledge about his patients? On the other hand, is it all right for the analyst not to have *any* knowledge of his patient's cultural background? Or does the truth, as it often does, lie somewhere in the middle?

And now comes the surprise. My analyst was very good—sensitive, insightful, patient. And I discovered that as my analysis progressed, my feelings of estrangement that had given rise to all the questions on cultural differences became fewer and fewer. What was happening? Was the cultural part of my self becoming less salient as the analysis touched ever-deeper layers of the self, as many psychoanalysts have claimed?

George Devereaux, a psychoanalyst who was also an anthropologist and a pioneer in addressing the issue of culture in psychoanalytic therapy, claimed that in really deep psychoanalytic therapy, the analyst needed to know the patient's specific cultural background less fully ahead of time than in more superficial forms of psychotherapy (Devereaux, 1953). In his conception of psychoanalysis as a universal, a-cultural science, the personality disorders that were the object of psychoanalysis represented a partial regression of (cultural) man to (universal) homo sapiens. 'For this reason,' he writes, 'children and abnormal members of our society resemble their counterparts in other cultures far more than the normal members of our society resemble the normal members of other ethnic groups.' (p. 632). A deep analysis would reveal the same universal fantasies and desires though, he allowed, the constellation of defense mechanisms could be culturally influenced.

In fact, for Devereaux, the most important (and harmful) influence exerted by culture on psychoanalytic therapy was not the analyst's indifference but his *interest* in cultural factors. He rightly pointed to the counter-transference danger of an analyst getting *too* interested in his analytic patient's culture. Sensitive to the analyst's interest, the patient would either gratify this interest by long discourses on his cultural practices or use these as red herrings to divert the analyst from probing deeper into his personal motivations. Freud is reputed to have sent a prospective patient, an Egyptologist, to another analyst because of Freud's own interest in Egyptology.

Most analysts have followed Devereaux's lead in maintaining that all those who seek help from a psychoanalyst have in common many fundamental and universal components in their personality structure. Together with the universality of the psychoanalytic method, these common factors sufficiently equip the analyst to understand and help his patient, irrespective of the patient's cultural background, a view reiterated by a panel of the American Psychoanalytic on the role of culture in psychoanalysis more than forty years ago (Jackson, 1968). There are certainly difficulties such as the ones enumerated by Ticho (1971) in treating patients of a different culture: a temporary impairment of the analyst's technical skills, empathy for the patient, diagnostic acumen, the stability of self and object representations, and the stirring up of counter-transference manifestations which may not be easily distinguishable from stereotypical reactions to the foreign culture. Generally, though, given the analyst's empathetic stance and the rules of analytic procedure, these difficulties are temporary and do not require a change in analytic technique. It is useful but not essential for the analyst to understand the patient's cultural heritage.

I believe that these conclusions on the role of culture in psychoanalytic therapy, which would seem to apply to my own experience, are superficially true but deeply mistaken. For what I did, and I believe most patients do, was to enthusiastically, if unconsciously, acculturate to the analyst's culture—in my case, both to his broader Western, north-European culture and to his particular Freudian psychoanalytic culture

My intense need to be 'understood' by the analyst, a need I shared with every patient, gave birth to an unconscious force that made me underplay those cultural parts of my self that I believed would be too foreign to the analyst's experience. Now, we know that every form of therapy is also an enculturation. As Fancher (1993) remarks: 'By the questions we ask, the things we empathize with, the themes we pick for our comment, the ways we conduct ourselves toward the patient, the language we use—by all these and a host of other ways, we communicate to the patient our notions of what is "normal" and normative. Our interpretations of the origins of a patient's issues reveal in pure form our assumptions of what causes what, what is problematic about life, where the patient did not get what s/he needed, what should have been otherwise' (pp. 89–90).

As a patient in throes of transference love, I was exquisitely attuned to the cues to my analyst's values, beliefs, and vision of the fulfilled life, which even the most non-intrusive of analysts cannot help but scatter during the therapeutic process. I was quick to pick up the cues that unconsciously shaped my reactions and responses accordingly, with their overriding goal to please and be pleasing in the eyes of the beloved. In the throes of what psychoanalysis calls 'transference-love', what I sought was closeness to the analyst, including the sharing of his culturally shaped interests, attitudes, and beliefs. This intense need to be close and to be understood, paradoxically by removing parts of the self from the analytic arena of understanding, was epitomized by the fact that I soon started dreaming in German, the language of my analyst, something I had neither done before my analysis nor have done after it.

The analysis being conducted in German fostered the excision of parts of my self. One's native tongue, the language of one's childhood, is intimately linked with emotionally coloured sensory-motor experiences. Psychotherapy in a language that is not the patient's own is often in danger of leading to 'operational thinking', that is verbal expressions lacking associational links with feelings, symbols, and memories (Basch-Kahre, 1984). However grammatically correct and rich in its vocabulary, the alien language suffers from emotional poverty, certainly as far as early memories are concerned. To give an example: there is often an impersonal tone characteristic of operational thinking when one of my bilingual patients reports significant experiences in English and much greater variations in affect when the same experience is described in Hindi, the patient's mother tongue. When in one of his sessions the patient reported, in English, that the previous night he had said to his wife, 'Let's have sex', his tone was detached, even slightly depressive. When asked what exactly he had said in Hindi, the answer was, '*teri le loon*' ('I'll take yours'). The much more concrete Hindi expression, demanding the use of the wife's vagina, objectifying the person, evoked in him not only greater feelings of an aggressive excitement (and shame while reporting it) but was also associated with fearful memories of childhood play when the same expression was directed at him by an older boy.

How should a Western psychoanalyst, then, approach the issue of cultural difference in his practice? The ideal situation would be that this difference exists only minimally, in the sense that the analyst has obtained a psychoanalytic knowledge of the patient's culture through a long immersion in its daily life and its myths, its folklore and literature, its language and its music—an absorption not through the bones as in case of his patient, but through the head and the heart. Anything less than this maximalist position has the danger of the analyst succumbing to the lure of cultural stereotyping in dealing with the particularities of the patient's experience. In cross-cultural therapeutic dyads, little knowledge is indeed a dangerous thing, collapsing important differences, assuming sameness when only similarities exist. What the analyst needs is not a detailed knowledge of the patient's culture but a serious questioning and awareness of the assumptions underlying his own, that is the culture he was born into and the culture in which he has been professionally socialized as a psychoanalyst. In other words, what I am suggesting is that in absence of the possibility of obtaining a psychoanalytic knowledge of his patient's culture, the analyst needs to strive for a state of affairs where the patient's feelings of estrangement because of his cultural differences from the analyst are minimized and the patient does not, or only minimally, cut off the cultural part of the self from the therapeutic situation. This is possible only if the analyst can convey a cultural openness which comes from becoming aware of his own culture's fundamental propositions about human nature, human experience, the fulfilled human life, and then to acknowledge their relativity by seeing them as cultural products, embedded in a particular place and time. He needs to become sensitive to the hidden existence of what Kohut (1979, p.12) called 'health and maturity moralities' of his particular analytical school. He needs to root out cultural judgments about what constitutes psychological maturity, gender-appropriate behaviours, 'positive' or 'negative' resolutions of developmental conflicts and complexes, that often appear in the garb of universally valid truths.

Given that ethnocentrism, the tendency to view alien cultures in terms of our own, and unresolved cultural chauvinism, are the patrimony of all human beings, including that of psychoanalysts, the acquisition of cultural openness is not an easy task. Cultural biases can lurk in the most unlikely places. For instance, psychoanalysts have traditionally accorded a high place to artistic creativity. To paint, sculpt, engage in literary and musical pursuits have not always and everywhere enjoyed the high prestige they do in modern Western societies. In other historical periods, many civilizations, including mine to this day, placed religious creativity at the top of their scale of desirable human endeavours. Psychoanalysts need to imagine that in such cultural settings, the following conclusion to a case report could be an example of a successful therapeutic outcome: 'The patient's visions increased markedly in quantity and quality and the devotional mood took hold of her for longer and longer periods of time.'

A therapist can evaluate his progress towards this openness by the increase in his feelings of curiosity and wonder when the cultural parts of the patient's self find their voice in therapy, when the temptation to pathologize the cultural part of his patient's behaviour decreases, when his own values no longer appear as normal and virtuous, and when his wish to instruct the patient in these values diminishes markedly. What about the cultural dilemmas of a non-Western analyst, such as myself, practising a Western discipline in an Asian country, a question I have often been asked? Psychoanalysis, we know, is informed by a vision of human experience that emphasizes man's individuality and his self-contained psyche. In the psychoanalytic vision, each of us lives in our own subjective world, pursuing pleasures and private fantasies, constructing a life and a fate that will vanish when our time is over. This view emphasizes the desirability of reflective awareness of one's inner states, an insistence that our psyches harbour deeper secrets than we care to confess, the existence of an objective reality that can be known, and an essential complexity and tragedy of life whereby many wishes are fated to remain unfulfilled. This vision is in contrast to my Hindu cultural heritage, which sees life not as tragic but as a romantic quest that can extend over many births, with the goal and possibility of apprehending another, 'higher' level of reality beyond the shared, verifiable, empirical reality of our world, our bodies, and our emotions. At the beginning of my practice in India, I was acutely aware of the struggle within myself between my inherited Indian culture and the

Freudian psychoanalytic culture that I had recently acquired and in which I had been professionally socialized. My romantic Indian vision of reality could not be reconciled with the ironic psychoanalytic vision, nor could the Indian view of the person and the sources of human strengths be reconciled with the Freudian view—now also mine—on the nature of the individual and his or her world. With Goethe's Faust, I could only say:

> Your spirit only seeks a single quest
> So never learns to know its brother
> Two souls, alas, dwell in my breast
> And one would gladly sunder from the other.

Some colleagues try to sunder the two souls by unreservedly identifying with their professional socialization, radically rejecting their Indian heritage. Many of them have migrated to Western countries to work as therapists, to all apparent purposes indistinguishable from their Western colleagues. Some who stay in India struggle to hold onto their professional identity by clinging to each psychoanalytic orthodoxy. Loath to be critical of received wisdom and exiled from Rome, they become more conservative than the Pope. Others, like myself, live with the oppositions, taking comfort from the Indian view that every contradiction does not need a resolution, that contradictions can co-exist in the mind like substances in water that are in suspension without necessarily becoming a solution.

I think I resolved this dilemma as do some men in Indian families who, after marrying, are caught up in the conflict between their mothers and wives, each asking the husband/son to choose between them. Unable to make this choice, the men often react by becoming detached from both. I found that the only way I could keep my affection for psychoanalytic and Hindu cultures intact was by loving each less—not by cutting myself off from one or the other but by engaging more critically with each. The loss of a certain measure of innocence and enthusiasm is the price paid for this strategy, a price that may not be too high for preventing a closing of the mind and for keeping intact a curiosity that is not satisfied with easy answers.

In conclusion, I would say that I do not doubt the universals of human nature. What I am pleading for is much more sensitive and careful delineation of what these universals actually are. Culture is not something that is a 'later' accretion to the psyche (in contrast to the notion of 'earlier' layers) or a matter of 'surface', in contrast to some imagined 'depths'. The culture in which an infant grows up, modern neurosciences tell us, constitutes the software of the brain, much of it already in place by the end of childhood. Not that the brain, a social and cultural organ as much as a biological one, does not keep changing with interactions with the environment in later life. Like the proverbial river, one never steps into twice, one never uses the same brain twice. Even if our genetic endowment were to determine 50 per cent of our psyche and early childhood experiences another 30 per cent, there is still a remaining 20 per cent that changes through the rest of our lives. Yet as the neurologist and philosopher Gerhard Roth (2006, p. 36) observes, 'Irrespective of its genetic endowment, a human baby growing up in Africa, Europe or Japan will become an African, a European or a Japanese. And once someone has grown up in a particular culture and, let us say, is 20 years old, he will never acquire a full understanding of other cultures since the brain has passed through the narrow bottleneck of "culturalization".'(My translation) As the anthropologist Clifford Geertz quipped on his fieldwork in Java, 'You are human only if you are a Javanese.'

REFERENCES

Bash-Kahre, E. (1984), 'On difficulties arising in transference and counter-transference when analyst and analysand have different socio-cultural backgrounds', *Int. Rev. of Psychoanalysis*: 61–7.

Devereaux, G. (1953), 'Cultural factors in psychoanalytic therapy', *Journal of American Psychoanalytic Association*, 1: 629–55.

Fancher, R.T. (1993), 'Psychoanalysis as culture', *Issues in Psychoanalytic Psychology*, 15(2): 81–93.

Jackson, S. (1968), 'Panel on aspects of culture in psychoanalytic theory and practice', *Journal of American Psychoanalytical Association*, 16: 651–70.

Kakar, S. (1978), *The Inner World: Childhood and Society in India*, Delhi: Oxford Univ. Press.

——— (1982), *Shamans, Mystics and Doctors*, New York: Knopf.

——— (1987), 'Psychoanalysis and non-western cultures', *Int. Rev. of Psychoanalysis*, 12: 441–8.

——— (1989), 'The maternal-feminine in Indian psychoanalysis', *Int. Rev. of Psychoanalysis*, 16(3): 355–62.

——— (1994), 'Clinical work and cultural imagination', *Psychoanalysis Quarterly*, 64: 265–81.

Kakar, S. and K. Kakar (2006), *The Indians: Portrait of a People*, Delhi: Penguin-Viking.

Kohut, H. (1979), 'The two analyses of Mr. Z', *Int. Journal of Psychoanalysis*, 60: 3–27.

Roth, G. (2006), *Die Zeit*, 23 Feburary.

Ticho, G. (1971), 'Cultural aspects of transference and counter-transference', *Bull. Meninger Clinic*, 35(5): 313–26.

3

Encounters of the Psychological Kind: Freud, Jung, and India

Freud's thought, and the method of treatment of emotional disorders he pioneered—psychoanalysis—arrived early in India. In fact, the Indian Psychoanalytic Society, formed in 1922, became a member of the International Psychoanalytic Association before such recognition was accorded to organized psychoanalysis in most European countries, for instance, France.

The moving spirit behind the reception of Freudian thought in India was Girindrasekhar Bose. Born in 1886 (Sinha, 1955; Hartnack, 1990), Bose was the son of the chief minister of a small princely state in Bengal. Although he studied medicine and practised as a physician in Calcutta after graduating in 1910, Bose's abiding intellectual passion was abnormal psychology. He learned hypnosis, and by 1914 he had begun to treat patients suffering from mental disorders by a technique closely akin, as he says, to Freud's original method, presumably the use of hypnosis, suggestion and questioning to recall memories and encourage associations. Before the first English translations of Freud's writings reached Calcutta making a strong impression on the young Bengali doctor's mind, he had already developed some of his psychological ideas. These included the basic elements of his theory of opposite wishes—namely that for every expressed wish there is an opposite wish working in the unconscious. A man of great energy and a good deal of originality, Bose immersed himself further in his psychological studies and in 1921 received the first doctor of science degree in psychology awarded in India. Steeped in Hindu philosophy and the Indian cultural tradition, Bose

Revised version of a paper first published in *The Psychoanalytic Study of Society*, 19, 1994.

had many other firsts to his credit: he held the first professorship of psychology at the University of Calcutta; he was a founder of the Indian Psychological Association; and, for us the most important, he was architect of the Indian Psychoanalytic Society.

The founder's meeting of the society took place in 1922 with Bose in the chair. Of the fifteen original members, nine were college teachers of psychology or philosophy, five—including two Britons—belonged to the medical corps of the Indian Army, and the professional affiliation of the remaining member is intriguingly listed as 'Secretary of the Jute Balers Association'. In the same year, Bose wrote to Freud in Vienna. After expressing sentiments of respect and admiration for the master's work, he informed him of the Indian Society. Freud was pleased that his ideas had spread to such a far-off land and asked Bose to write to Ernest Jones, then President of the International Psychoanalytical Association, for membership in that body. Bose did so and the Indian Psychoanalytic Society, with Bose as its first President—a position he was to hold till his death in 1953—became a full-fledged member of the international psychoanalytic community.

Cut off from the thrust and parry of debate, controversy, and ferment of the psychoanalytic centres in Europe, dependent on books and journals that were not easily available for intellectual sustenance, Indian psychoanalysis was nurtured through its infancy primarily by the enthusiasm and intellectual passion of its progenitor. Informal meetings with eight to ten people were held on Saturday evenings at the president's house—the house was to become the headquarters of the Indian Society after Bose's death. Bose read most of the papers and led almost all the discussions. Without the benefit of training analysis himself, it was Bose who 'analysed' the other members in a more or less informal manner and otherwise endeavoured to keep their enthusiasm for psychoanalysis alive. In the 20s, psychoanalysis intrigued the Western-educated Bengali elite of Calcutta, Freud's concepts being popularized through radio broadcasts and magazine articles (Hartnack, 1990). Analytic theory was seen as an intriguing new tool for the analysis of Indian culture and social phenomena. Even Gandhi, in his search for a solution to the perpetual Hindu-Muslim problem, attended a meeting of the Psychoanalytic Society in Calcutta in 1925 at which one of the British members of the society, Berkeley-Hill, presented a psychoanalytic analysis of the tension between Hindus and Muslims.

From my own experience of psychoanalytic institutes in different countries I would venture to say that the practice of psychoanalysis is not unlike that of the performance of Indian classical music where the basic musical vocabulary may be shared, yet each *gharana* or school of music has a specific, traditional way of elaborating and performing a *raga*. The musician has learnt this traditional way through personal instruction over many years from his teacher who, in turn, has learnt it from his teacher and so on. Similarly, the way we practise psychoanalysis is essentially learnt from our own training analysis and can often be traced to a particular psychoanalytic *gharana*. Such a *gharana* is not to be confused with a self-conscious school advancing a divergent theoretical position. All it means is that the practitioners belonging to a *gharana* share a particular style of psychoanalytic 'performance'. Coterminous with a training institute or even with a national boundary, the *gharana*'s original teacher can often be traced back to the first generation of analysts.

In any event, because of its relative isolation, Indian psychoanalytic practice has been decisively marked by the stamp of the first Indian analyst. Essentially, Bose's method is derived from the psychiatric practice of his pre-Freudian years, his theory of opposite wishes and his readings of Freud's writings on analytic technique. In a short communication to the *International Journal of Psychoanalysis* (Bose, 1931), he described it as follows:

In contrast with the active therapy and the forced fantasy method of Ferenczi, the method has the following salient features.

In suitable cases the patient is first asked to give his free associations to determine the nature of the repressed wish active at the time. He is then *ordered* [itals. mine] to build up wish fulfillments and fantasies with reference to the repressed wish, ultimately taking up the roles of the subject and the object in the wish-situation.

The patient was further instructed to repeat this at home and to report the resultant fantasies in the next analytic hour. In session the patient reclined in an easy chair with his eyes closed, the analyst sitting at the back diligently taking notes of what he or she said.

These detailed notes were more than an *aid-memoire* for the analyst. They were actively used in the process of analysis for breaking down resistance. 'The record is of value also in removing the resistances of the patient who may be denying some of his former statements in spite of the assertions of the analyst to the contrary. A reference to notes brings about a conviction of the truth of interpretations much more' (Bose, 1948). As late as in 1966, the brochure published on the occasion of the silver jubilee celebrations of Lumbini Park, the mental hospital run by the

Indian Society, shows in its photographic illustration of an analytic session, a patient sitting with his eyes closed on a folding canvas chair while the analyst behind him is bent over a notebook writing down his utterances.

When Bose instructs the patient on the direction his fantasy should take, he is not far removed from some of the meditative procedures used in the Hindu psycho-philosophical schools of self-realization. Tantrik visualization such as *nyasa* or the *Yoganidra* of Raja Yoga come immediately to mind. They are techniques with which Bose, through his deep study of Yoga, was thoroughly familiar.

Many may have grave reservations about the content of the clinical material elicited by the active, didactic stance of the Indian analyst, a stance to which the analytic method of Bose has greatly contributed. One can legitimately wonder if the analyst's activity does not come perilously close to what a lawyer is forbidden to do in the courtroom, namely 'lead the witness', increasing the chances of suggestion and thus adulterating the clinical data beyond salvation.

We know that ever since Freud, who was seriously concerned about the suggestion problem, analysts have tried to make sure that analytic technique, in contrast to other psychotherapies, minimizes suggestion to an extent where it can no longer be regarded as an alternative explanation. As Marshall Edelson reminds us, the bulk of analytic interventions in the clinical situation comprises interpreting the defence rather than suggesting what the patient is defending against, intervening by calling attention to the patient's habitual way of resolving ambiguities in life and in the analytic situation, pointing out the context in which the analysand has difficulties in saying what he has on his mind, and calling attention to what needs further explanation (Edelson, 1984). Such interventions are relatively free from the taint of suggestion. Heightened didactic activity on the part of the analyst thus need not be *ipso facto* suggestive. The analyst can exhort, encourage and interact as much as demanded by the context in which he operates, as long as he refrains from suggesting the contents of a defence or of an unconscious conflict till the patient himself discovers it in some form or other. The *public* record of raw data in psychoanalysis being notoriously limited, we have no way of knowing whether the pioneers of the Indian *gharana* (or, for that matter, of any other school) rigorously followed the discipline of the analytic technique. We also have no overriding reason to doubt that they did not.

Well into the 1940s, the published work of Indian psychoanalysts shows a persisting concern with the illumination of Indian cultural phenomena as well as registers the 'Indian' aspects of their patients' mental life. Mythological allusions to Hindu gods and goddesses like Shiva or Kali regularly crop up in case-history reports where the mythology appears to be used by the patient for both defensive and adaptive purposes. Thus, for instance, T. C. Sinha, a student of Bose and later himself a president of the Indian Society, reports the case of a sixteen-year old youth whose intense passive homosexual wishes were accompanied by the fear of pregnancy. He countered the analyst's reassurance that men could not become pregnant by referring to the example of the mythical Yuvanasva. Though he had a hundred wives, the king Yuvanasva had no son and approached sages for remedy. Taking pity on him they performed a special ritual. A jug of water was made potent by recitals of mantras to be given to the queens to make them pregnant. Unknowingly, Yuvanasva drank of this water and after ten months gave birth to a child who came out of his body by bursting open the right side of his stomach. To protect himself from Yuvanasva's mythical fate, the patient now developed the fantasy of having his own penis inside his anus (Sinha, 1949).

We come across papers on the Hindu psychology of expiation, on the interpretation—in the light of *Totem* and *Taboo*—of *prasad*, that is, the food remains that of God or a superior person. There are studies of Indian sculptural motifs such as the *lingam, ardhanarishwara*, and *Mahisasura-mardini* as representing various aspects of the oedipal situation in the Hindu family in the light of psychoanalytic theory We also encounter scattered comparative observations such as 'The Indian paranoiac often turns to religion.'

By the 1940s, however, the interest in comparative and cultural aspects of mental life, as well as the freshness of writing by the pioneering generation of Indian psychoanalysts was lost. In the last twenty-five years, to judge from the official journal of the Indian Society, Indian contributions have been neither particularly distinctive nor original. Even the best papers are little more than status reports on global analytic concepts or introduction to the theories of a few selected post-Freudians such as Klein or Bion.[1]

Here I can only speculate on the reasons for this total divorce of Indian psychoanalysis from Indian culture and society. Psychoanalysis, in the

---

[1] It is thus to the credit of the Indian Society that its journal has been continuously published since 1948. As a visiting colleague remarked, 'It is not how well a bear dances but that it dances at all.'

sense of psychoanalytic concepts and theories which gain a large number of adherents among analysts at a given time and subsequently shape their clinical observations, is not completely independent of the historical situation of the analyst and his patients. Freud's postulation of the death instinct and increasing interest in the problems of human aggression after the carnage of the First World War, the magnified importance of object-relations theories after the reassertions and renaissance of the values of the Counter-Enlightenment in Western societies since the late 1960s, are only two instances of the influence of the historical Zeitgeist on theorizing and practice.

In India, the last forty years have witnessed an ever-increasing pace of modernization and industrialization. The country has entered in a big way into the world market, both economic and intellectual, which is dominated by the First World. There has been a phenomenal rise of an urban, educated middle class to which normally both the Indian analysts and their patients belong. A consequence of these related processes has been the uncritical acceptance by the middle class, itself the child of modernization, of Western intellectual models (of which Marxism is also one) with claims to universality. It is perhaps no accident that in Bombay, the most Western of Indian cities, both geographically and spiritually, the younger generation of psychoanalysts are adherents of the Kleinian school which, with its focus on the universal aspects of the object—'good' and 'bad' breasts, 'good' and 'bad' penises and so on—is perhaps the most universalistic of the many 'relational' theories. But even in traditional Calcutta on the eastern sea coast, any critical engagement with received theory has by now almost disappeared. This was not true of the early period of psychoanalysis in India. If psychoanalysis is any kind of illustration for the rest of Indian intellectual life, then it seems that when India entered the world market on a truly large scale after Independence, the Western colonialization of the Indian mind paradoxically became greater than was the case when the country was still a British colony.

The absence of the cultural idiom in the case histories today, such as the patient's use of Indian mythology, are then not only due to presumed increase in mythological illiteracy as a consequence of the modernizing process; it may well be due to the patient's sensing the analyst's disinterest in such material because of his commitment to 'deeper' universalistic models. Far from the intellectual founts of his professional existence, practising in a culture indifferent to psychoanalytic ideas and hostile to its view of the person, the Indian analyst may be tempted to idealize analytic 'gurus' in distant, presumably more receptive lands, and uncritically follow their models in the smallest details.

What are the reasons for the Indian rejection of, or rather indifference to, Freud and psychoanalytic thought? Before I begin to formulate an answer, I must emphasize that I am not going to deal with the rejection of psychoanalytic therapy as a method of treatment of emotional disorders, a subject that has been competently discussed by others (Zwiebel, 1991). My focus here will be on the rejection of psychoanalytic ideas that in the West have been often employed as powerful tools in the service of a radical cultural critique.

At first glance, the Indian hostility to psychoanalysis seems surprising, given the fact that there has rarely been a civilization in human history that has concerned itself so persistently, over the millennia, with the nature of the 'self' and with seeking answers to the question, 'Who am I?' As a colonized people, however, reeling under the onslaught of a conquering Western civilization that proclaimed its forms of knowledge and its political and social structures as self-evidently superior, Indian intellectuals in the early twentieth century felt the need to cling doggedly to at least a few distinctive Indian forms in order to maintain intact their civilization's identity. The Indian concern with the 'self', its psycho-philosophical schools of 'self-realization', often appearing under the label of Indian metaphysics or 'spirituality', became one of the primary ways of salvaging self-respect, even a means of affirming a superiority over a materialistic Western civilization. Psychoanalysis was then a direct challenge to the Indian intellectual's important source of self-respect; it stepped on a turf the Indian felt was uniquely his own. In his comments on Freudian theory, Sri Aurobindo, an influential mystic-philosopher, exemplified this trend when he wrote: '. . . one cannot discover the meaning of the lotus by analyzing the secrets of the mud in which it grows.' He also stated that psychoanalysis as a science is 'still in its infancy—inconsiderate, awkward and rudimentary at one and the same time' (Kakar, 1982, p. 121). These sentiments have been echoed by others and still characterize the attitude of many Indian intellectuals, even of those who are not professionally engaged with Indian philosophy.

Another reason for the rejection of Freudian concepts had to do with their origins. Derived from clinical experience, with patients growing up in a cultural environment very different from the one in India, some of the transposed concepts often did not carry much conviction. As we saw in the example of Bose, the different patterns of family life and the role of multiple caretakers in India pushed in the direction of modifications of psychoanalytical theory. Similarly, Freudian views of religion, derived from the Judeo-Christian monotheistic tradition, with its emphasis on a father-god, had little reverence for the Indian religious tradition of polytheism, where mother-goddesses often constituted the deepest sub-stratum of Indian religiosity.

As far as the other side of the equation is concerned, the effect of India or Indian thought on Freud was minimal or even nonexistent. Although his correspondence with Indian analysts such as Bose is polite, Freud was fundamentally disinterested in Indian cultural particularities that might press toward any revision or questioning of his hard-won concepts. It also did not help that Bose had developed an idiosyncratic version of the basic free association method that came dangerously close to the psycho-analytic sin of suggestion. India and Indian thought, such as its mystic-ism, was the indirect occasion of one of Freud's works, *Civilization and its Discontents*, which he wrote in response to a letter from Romain Rolland. Rolland had sought Freud's views on the mystical experience, 'the oceanic feeling', both his own and that of the nineteenth-century Bengali mystic Ramakrishna, whose biography he was working on at the time. Freud (1930) stated his attitude towards India and things Indian concisely when he wrote: 'I shall now try with your guidance to pene-trate into the Indian jungle from which until now an uncertain blend-ing of Hellenic love of proportion, Jewish sobriety, and Philistine timidity have kept me away' (p. 392). A historian of Indian psycho-analysis attributes Freud's attitude towards India, his disinterest in an intercultural exchange that could go beyond a mere confirmation of his own 'expansionist strivings', to his being a man of his (colonial) times. Christiane Hartnack (1990) writes: 'His work on women and other cul-tures reflected prominent stereotypes of his time by presupposing that European men are the measure to which all human beings are to be com-pared. Thus, just as Freud was too bound by the social norms of his time to overcome the then contemporary misogynistic views, he did not ques-tion European hegemonic attitudes, and so his psychoanalysis remained eurocentric' (pp. 948–9).

As a psychoanalyst, however, I would go beyond Hartnack's political explanation and complement it with a psychological one to discern in Freud's reaction to the Indian jungle some unconscious, life-historical determinants. Freud has taught us that an individual's passionately held convictions and ideas are not autonomous from his unconscious needs and conflicts, and we should not hesitate to apply this lesson to Freud himself. The Indian jungle, I believe, was for Freud the lushness of his mother's body, Indian mysticism, the siren song of the eternal feminine, which was to remain a source of ambivalence for Freud through much of his life. 'Oh, you Indians with your eternal mother complex!' he is reported to have exasperatedly remarked to an Indian patient who had sought him out for consultations (Anand, 1990). Freud's ambivalence towards the maternal is also reflected in the directions taken by his work. Until well into the mid-1930s, Freud's writings did not take the infant's early experience of its mother fully into account, though towards the end, his recognition of the impact of the mother on mental life was coming closer to conscious toleration. The ambivalence towards the maternal–feminine began to ease as he himself was being inexorably pulled into the embrace of the *ewig Weilblich*.

In contrast to Freud, Jung's involvement with Indian thought was deep and extensive and influenced his work although, as we shall see later, the nature and the extent of influence has often been overestimated by Indian intellectuals. Although Jung, after his break with Freud, had been a student of Yoga—and for Jung, we must remember, 'Yoga' is a general term for all Eastern religious thought and psychological practice—his major writings on Indian, and generally Eastern, religions took place between 1936 and 1944. A part of Jung's attraction to Indian thought had to do with his feud with Freud. Yoga, Jung felt, confirmed his position that there is more to the unconscious than sexual libido. India was thus an ally in his effort to prevent Western psychology from becoming a hostage to Freud's sexual theories. Although Yoga played a role in stimulating his awareness and perhaps contributing to some of his insights, it was, above all, a field for appropriation in the sense that Jung took from it parallels that confirmed his own theories. As Harold Coward (1985) writes: 'The principle of finding confirmation in form, rather than content, of psychic experience, typifies most of Jung's contact with Yoga' (p. 7). Some of the psychological concepts of Yoga that Jung found common and thus incorporated in his own theorizing are *citta*, with its parallel to the Jungian psyche, *tapas* and what Jung calls 'active imagination', *guru* and 'thought beings', *atman* and the Jungian self, *samskaras* and the 'archetypes', especially *mandala*, as the pre-eminent archetype of wholeness.

Jung, however, was at pains to distinguish his own work from Indian mystical and religious thought, often by dismissing the latter as non-scientific, speculative, and metaphysical while emphasizing his own scientific empiricism. In one of his letters to an Indian correspondent Jung (1953) wrote:

My conceptions are empirical and not at all speculative. If you understand them from a philosophical standpoint you go completely astray, since they are not rational but mere names of groups of irrational phenomena. The conceptions of Indian philosophy, however, are thoroughly philosophical and have the character of postulates and can therefore only be analogous to my terms but not identical with them.

Analytic psychology tells you the story of his (modern European man's) adventures. Only if you are able to see the relativity, i.e., the uncertainty of all human postulates, can you experience that state in which analytical psychology makes sense. But analytical psychology just makes no sense for you.

Nothing of the things I describe comes to life unless you can accompany or sympathize understandingly with beings that are forced to base their life upon facts to be experienced and not transcendental postulates beyond human experience. Thus, in as much as you are a believer in postulates, you have no use for my psychology and you are not even able to understand why we shouldn't simply adopt Indian philosophy if we are dissatisfied with our religious philosophy (pp. 302–3).

And to another correspondent he wrote (Jung, 1953):

I know it is a special feature of Indian thought that consciousness is assumed to have a metaphysical and prehuman existence . . . as far as my knowledge goes, however, we have no evidence at all in favor of the hypothesis that a prehuman and preconscious psyche is conscious to anybody and therefore a consciousness . . . the Western mind has renounced metaphysical assertions which are *per definitionem* nor verifiable, if only recently so. In the Middle Ages up to the 19th century, we still believed in the possibility of metaphysical assertions. India, it seems to me, is still convinced of the possibility of metaphysical assertions. Perhaps she is right and perhaps she is not (pp. 254–5).

Jung did admire India but the admiration was for the Indian as a civilized 'noble savage' possessing certain vital sensibilities that the Westerner could be nostalgic about but which he could no longer directly adopt. These sensibilities were the harvest of a field different from the one Western civilization had chosen to cultivate. Jung (1970) was to write after his visit to India in 1938:

Indian life is unimaginably rich in color and detail, but it seems essentially transitory, dreamlike, because it gives expression to the unconscious world that the Westerner denies. Indians do not think like Westerners but to perceive their thoughts, similar to primitive thought processes, a natural development of a civilization that brought every essential trace of primitivity with it (p. 525).

'Yoga', or Indian metaphysical and psychological thought, was then essentially incompatible with the Western mind and could be even harmful if its teachings and methods were taken over directly.

'Yoga, to me,' he wrote in a letter (Jung, 1953), 'is no more than a subject of research. It neither impresses me or deceives me. During my stay in India I saw for myself that Yoga is not at all what we think. The Hatha Yoga is more often no more than aerobatics, or simply gymnastics; or else it is a physiological aid to concentration, an aid which these highly emotional people need very much in order to master themselves' (p. 310). Jung's trip to India, on which he contracted amoebic dysentery, strengthened his ambivalence toward the subcontinent, its metaphysical thought, and even its mystics. While in Madras, a meeting with Ramana Maharishi, one of the greatest Indian mystics of this century, had been arranged, but by that time Jung 'was so involved with the obvious Maya of this world that I didn't care anymore if there had been twelve Maharishis on top of each other' (p. 478).

And like any other Western tourist he was impatient with what he perceived to be Indian indifference to the problems and tasks of the pre-sent. Commenting on Parmahansa Yogananda's *Autobiography of a Yogi*, he writes (Jung, 1953): '100 per cent pure coconut oil, standing at 105° F in shade and 100 per cent humidity . . . unsurpassed as an antidote to disastrous population explosion and traffic jams and the threat of spiritual starvation, so rich in vitamins that albumen, carbohydrates, and such like banalities become supererogatory . . . Happy India! Halcyon coconut palm-fringed elephantiasis isles, chuppaties reeking of hot oil—oh my liver can't bear them anymore!' (pp. 42–3).

In various places in his writings and letters, Jung has characterized the Indian (i.e. the Hindu) as soft, passive, and feminine whereas the European is hard, active, and masculine. He contrasts the intuitive and introverted Indian with the scientific and extroverted Western man. The Indian lives in a timeless world, unconcerned with reality and history whereas the European's world is its opposite. Indian consciousness is exclusively matriarchal whereas Western consciousness has undergone a differentiation of the parental images: it has both a father and a mother though it may have dispossessed the latter. India, for Jung, became the psychic opposite of Europe, the unconscious of the West, and the Indian a cartoon of everything a European was not—a caricature regarded with affection, even admiration, but a caricature nevertheless.

The question is not whether Jung was right or wrong in his appraisal of Indian cultural psychology. My caveat is that he arrived at his conclusions not through his much-vaunted empiricism, that is, through a long engagement with the mental productions of Indian patients or with the products of Indian cultural imagination such as myths, legends, and tales, but through the operation and needs of a hegemonic European consciousness that found a home in India for all that was felt to be lost in Europe. India, for Jung, was a black mirror in which European man glimpses himself darkly, but a mirror nevertheless, an object to be used, appropriated when necessary, but not a subject in its own right. Like sexist discourse, which either looks down at women as whores or elevates them to untouchable goddesses, the colonialist psychological discourse also dismissed non-Western people either as irrational, less-differentiated primitives or elevated them to a class of noble savages, close to unconscious rhythms of life and nature and possessors of an intuitive wisdom. Whereas Freud can be said to exemplify the former tendency, Jung is clearly the representative of the latter; both were part of their colonial times and were influenced by the European hegemonic ideology.

Indian intellectuals reacted to Jung's professed admiration for their traditional thought and to his pointing at parallels between his psychology and 'Yoga' with appreciation and pride. Jung's views were a much needed bolstering of nationalistic self-esteem, a valued source of narcissistic enhancement. Universities closely identified with India's national aspirations—Benares, Allahabad, and Calcutta—plied Jung with honorary degrees and he was much fêted during the course of his Indian sojourn. Unlike the Freudian school, though, Jungian psychology could not establish itself as a therapeutic system in India. There is no institutional structure that trains practitioners in the craft of Jungian therapeutics and, with a solitary exception, there have been no trained practising Jungian analysts in any city. In the pursuit of their own anticolonial agenda, Indian intellectuals felt that Jung had confirmed the 'truth' of Indian metaphysics, a source of their 'superiority' over the West. In this endeavour, they ignored (as they continue to do to this day) Jung's ambivalence and grave reservations about Indian thought. Just as Freud and Jung had appropriated India for their own purposes, Jung was appropriated by Indian intellectuals for their concerns about the preservation of an Indian identity and in service of their polemics against Western hegemonic strivings.

Viewing Freud and Jung through anticolonial glasses, polished anew by modern theories of deconstructionism, Indians by and large rejected Freud's theories and chose to regard Jung's psychology as a homage. In both cases, however, a serious engagement with the contents of the psychologies, as they relate or run counter to traditional Indian thought and psychology, together with a careful sifting of the available empirical evidence, rarely took place. Genuine encounters between Western and Indian psychology, free of a hidden colonial discourse on one side and anticolonial polemical intention on the other, have yet to take place. Looking at the current upsurge of Third World national and ethnic consciousness, the possibility of such an encounter appears to be more remote than it did even 20 years ago.

REFERENCES

Anand, M. R. (1990), Personal Conversation, 12 December.

Bose, G. (1931), 'A New Technique of Psychoanalysis', *Int. Journal of Psychoanalysis*, 12, 387–8.

———— (1948), 'A New Theory of Mental Life', *Samiksa* 2, 108–205.

Coward, H. (1985), *Jung and Eastern Thought*, Albany, NY: State Univ. of New York Press.

Edelson, M. (1984), 'Hypothesis and Evidence in Psychoanalysis', Chicago: Univ. of Chicago Press.

Freud, S. (1930), 'Letter to Romain Rolland', 19 January 1930, in E. Freud ed., *The Letters of Sigmund Freud*, New York Basic Books, p. 392.

Hartnack, C. (1990), 'Vishnu on Freud's Desk: Psychoanalysis in Colonial India', *Social Research*, 57: 921–49.

Jung, C. G. (1953), *Letters*, vol. 2, Princeton, NJ: Princeton Univ. Press.

———— (1970), *Collected Works*, vol. 10, Princeton, NJ: Princeton Univ. Press.

Kakar, S. (1982), *Shamans, Mystics and Doctors*, New York: A. Knopf.

———— (1989), 'Stories from Indian Psychoanalysis: Context and Text', in J. Stigler, R. Shweder and G. Herdt eds, *Cultural Psychology*, New York: Cambridge Univ. Press, pp. 427–45.

Sinha, T. C. (1966), 'Development of Psychoanalysis in India', *Int. Journal of Psychoanalysis*, 47: 427–39.

———— (1949), 'Some Psychoanalytical Observations on the Siva Linga', *Samiksa* 3.

4

Psychoanalysis and
Non-Western Cultures

Historically, the relationship between psychoanalysis and non-Western cultures has not been particularly satisfactory. In spite of his wide-ranging cultural interests, Freud was generally indifferent to all that lay outside the Western intellectual and artistic tradition. And for obvious reasons, Jung's enthusiasm for the East had more the effect of dampening rather than increasing psychoanalytic involvement in the major non-Western traditions.

Psychoanalytic interest in non-Western cultures, then, has not only been limited but its occasional manifestations have displayed one or the other of two characteristics. First, in the early years of its development, when psychoanalysis was concerned with claiming and defending the universality of its findings, it strove mightily to be the foremost proponent of the classic 'psychic unity of mankind' position. Re-reading the early papers of various aspects of non-Western cultures, it is apparent that psychoanalytic engagement with these cultures was of an appropriating kind, as territories to be annexed, particularly for the Oedipus complex. Given the self-image of the pioneering generation of analysts as being conquistadors and embattled at the same time, the psychoanalytic encounter with other cultures could not be one of mutual learning and collaborative inquiry into human existence. The paramount concern of psychoanalysis seems to have been in protecting and gathering evidence in support of its key concepts rather than in entertaining the possibility that other cultures, with their different world-views, family structures and relationships, could contribute to its models and concepts. In many ways, Geza Roheim's (1945, 1950) wide-ranging and scholarly inquiry

First published in *International Review of Psychoanalysis*, 12, 1985, 441–8. Reprinted with the permission of the Institute of Psychoanalysis, London.

into other cultures exemplifies this particular thrust. Using Freud's theories as proven scientific laws like those of physics (*Komplex natur-wissen-schaftlich abgesicherten Gesetzaussagen*), Roheim tried to show that in fables and dreams, in rituals and artistic creations of different cultures, the same infantile fantasies were operative and the same symbols and mythical figures appeared and reappeared.

The second feature of the analytic encounter with non-Western cultures has more to do with its clinical aspect than with the preservation of its theoretical postulates. With its well-defined goals of mental health—even when it concedes that these are ideal goals to be striven for rather than achieved—early psychoanalysis had a rather determined view of the 'healthy personality', the 'genital character', or the 'mature person'. The healthy and neurotic distinction was soon applied to whole communities, as in the writings of George Devereux and his followers (Devereux, 1956; Masson, 1980). Predictably, non-Western cultures were bunched more at the neurotic end of the spectrum and *their* soul-doctors, the shamans, were evaluated as frankly psychotic (Boyer, 1962).

The sanction for the extension of the concept of neurosis from individuals to cultures was once again derived from Freud's work, though Freud was considerably more careful and circumspect in his own pronouncements on the issue. Thus in 'Civilization and its Discontents' (1930) he writes: 'the diagnosis of communal neuroses is faced with a special difficulty. In an individual neurosis we take as our starting-point the contrast that distinguishes the patient from his environment, which is assumed to be 'normal'. For a group all of whose members are affected by one and the same disorder no such background could exist; it would have to be found elsewhere . . . But in spite of all these difficulties, we may expect that one day someone will venture to embark upon a pathology of cultural communities' (p. 144). Some analysts indeed did embark on the venture of constructing such cultural pathologies. In this enterprise they took, it appears, the middle-class man of north-European and north-American societies as the yardstick for measuring the neurotic deviations of people growing up in non-Western cultures.

The results, to put it mildly, have not been encouraging. To take my own society, India, as an example, according to most of these writings, oral fixation and oral dependence have never been quite surmounted and the resolution of the oedipal complex among Indians has never been quite accepted (Daly, 1927; Mitchell, 1957). In one of the more recent contributions (Silvan, 1981) Indian behaviour patterns have been explained 'as the result of intense libidinal gratification throughout the oral, anal and phallic exhibitionistic phases, in continuation with stringent restraints on aggression, followed by overstimulation in the oedipal period and subsequent harsh frustrations during latency. This specific sequence requires strong defensive measures, particularly against sadism, and favours reaction formation. Most especially there is a pull to oral fixation . . . Rigid proscriptions around eating and killing animals suggest reaction formation. Oral eroticism is seen in cultural emphasis on generosity, especially around food, institutionalized dependency, totalism, etc.' (p. 97).

Leaving aside the fact that most of the observations raise doubts whether their authors possess a sufficiently detailed and nuanced knowledge of Indian culture and society to make interpretations which are empathic and phenomenologically sensitive, there are some fundamental issues involved in such psychoanalytic ventures into non-Western cultures. First, it is difficult to comprehend the basis on which gratification in another culture is judged as intense or inadequate, a stimulation as 'over' or 'under', a frustration harsh or mild. Behind the seemingly innocuous adjectives lie cultural assumptions and attitudes which are fused with scientific explanation. Let me illustrate this through examples.

We know that in general, from the moment of birth, the Indian infant is greeted and surrounded by direct, sensual body contact, by relentless physical ministrations (Kakar, 1978; Roland, 1980). Constantly cuddled in the mother's arms, the baby's experience of the mother's body is a heady one. When the infant is a few months old and able to rest on his stomach, he may be carried astride the mother's hip, his legs on each side of her body, as she goes about on visits to neighbours, to the market, to the fields and on other errands. At other times (and in other places) the infant may also be carried in a similar way against the stomach or against the back of the mother or her substitute. For many years the child will sleep at night with the mother in the same bed, shifting to the bed of some other family member only when the maternal bed has become too crowded, say, after the birth of a third child. Patients who have slept with their mothers till the onset of puberty are not uncommon in Indian analytic practice. The mother's (or her substitute's) smell, body warmth and the texture of her skin, in a climate which ensures that a minimum or no clothing at all is worn by the young child, pervade the early sensory experience of most Indians.

There are other sources of specifically sexual, genital excitement embedded in the culture's customs and material conditions. As Sinha (1977) has pointed out, in villages people tie a black or red thread around a young child's waist, just over the hip bones. From this thread copper coins or small conch shells are usually suspend which touch the pelvic region, acting as genital stimulants. Moreover, since in most Indian homes parents and children sleep and in fact live in one room, the opportunities for the child to witness parental coitus are common. The sexual excitement caused by these occasions, since often repeated, becomes integrated and is normally not a source of intolerable disturbance. In other words, the primal scene, in being a long running play, is not the momentous event it appears in the analyses of Western middle-class patients with their very different living conditions, notions of privacy and the mystification around the 'parental bedroom'.

The greater sensual stimulation and sexual excitement of the child is, then, simply a part of growing up in India and from the Indian point of view the assertion that a European or American child is sensually starved or under-stimulated, is as valid as the opposite observation from a Western perspective. In such matters, it is necessary for analysts engaged with other cultures in the clinical or research situation to recall Erikson's (1963) statement: 'While it is quite clear, then, what *must* happen to keep the baby alive (the minimum supply necessary) and what *must not* happen, lest he die or be severely stunted (the maximum frustration tolerable), there is increasing leeway in regard to what may happen; and different cultures make extensive use of their prerogative to decide what they consider workable and insist on calling necessary' (p. 68).

My second example is related to an issue in analytic technique, namely, the concept of analytic neutrality, Freud's 'blank screen' or 'reflecting mirror' (Freud, 1912). For the non-Western analyst, the analytic neutrality has to be interpreted and practised in the context of the broader communication patterns of his culture. In India, the cultural pattern requires that irrespective of the nature of the patient's psychopathology, the analyst be much more actively involved than may be considered desirable in the classical model.

There are many reasons why in India the analyst's humaneness, sympathy and therapeutic intent cannot be subtly conveyed in an atmosphere of reserved formality but need a more open and active expression. First, as I have pointed out elsewhere (Kakar, 1982) it is rarely recognized how much a certain kind of introspection—a *sine qua non* for psychoanalysis—is a peculiarly Western trait, deeply rooted in Western philosophical and literary traditions. As Simon and Weiner (1966) have shown, the introspective element of Western civilization is ancient and can be traced back to later Greek thought where the definitions of self and of identity became contingent upon an active process of examining, sorting out and scrutinizing the 'events' and 'adventures' of one's own life. The activity of introspection became closely connected with the idea of 'the true self', as typified by the Socratic use of the phrase 'Know thyself'. This kind of introspection is simply not a feature of Indian culture and its literary traditions. Even today, in the essentially Western inspired genre of autobiography, Indian writings often tend to have a curiously flat quality as far as the scrutiny of the life in terms an examination of motives and feelings are concerned. With rare exceptions, Indian autobiographies are evocations of places and accounts of careers; records of events from which the self has been excised. This observation is not meant to be a criticism but to point out the absence of an Indian counterpart to Western-style introspection. The meditative procedures of Indian psycho-philosophical schools of 'self-realization' to which introspective activity may conceivably be compared, are of a different nature and follow radically different goals. The Indian injunction 'Know thy Self' (*atamanam vidhi*) is related to a self other than the one referred to by Socrates. It is a self uncontaminated by time and space and thus without the life historical dimension which is a focus of psychoanalysis and of Western romantic literature. In some of the best modern Indian novels, the introspective passages are generally hesitant and unsure, the look inward often coming to rest upon the self of Indian philosophy rather than the self of a uniquely personal psychology. Let me add that I am speaking here in broad cultural-historical terms and not referring to introspective capacities of particular individuals in India or, for that matter, in the West, which may vary widely across the spectrum. My general impression of Indian patients who do not belong to the Westernized upper class or to the reflective members of the traditional elite is that the 'psychological mindedness' which is held to be one of the criteria for analysability is a rare occurrence.

An Indian analyst must confront the fact that for most of his patients, emotional problems do not have a life historical dimension or, even more generally, a genesis in the 'psyche'. If not attributed to possession by malevolent or unsatisfied spirits who definitely lie *outside* the individual, the disorders and conflicts are often seen as the product of the *karma* of a previous life. Thus a woman in her early thirties, becoming aware of her aggressive impulses toward her husband as revealed in a dream, spontaneously exclaimed, 'Ah, these are due to my *samskaras* (the karmic traces from a past life). However hard I try to be a good wife, my bad *samskaras* prevent me.' Introspection in the Western sense thus may often have to be taught and so an Indian analyst is often necessarily more actively didactical than his Western colleague.

In addition, traditional child rearing practices and the ideology of social relations emphasize a demostratively close 'symbiotic' mode of relating with significant others (Kakar, 1978; Roland, 1980). The demonstration of compassion and interest, warmth and responsiveness expected of the analyst by the Indian analysand is generally nearer to what he would expect from a professional doctor—the model that pervades analyses in the West. An Indian analyst, if he wants to keep his patients, cannot ignore these cultural expectations and must carve out his analytic neutrality within the parameters set by them. Furthermore, the emphasis on analytic communication through words is counter to the dominant Indian idiom in which words are only a small part of a vast store of signs and semiotics. The pitch and intonation of voice, facial expressions, hand gestures and bodily movements are expected to play a large role in any close interpersonal encounter. These too are expectations to which the Indian analyst, given his own embeddedness in the idiom of the culture, is not immune.

Perhaps it is clear from my examples that in arguing for a relativizing of psychoanalysis through an inquiry into non-Western experience, I do not question the great developmental constants psychoanalysis has uncovered. These are, of course, based on a shared, universal experience of infancy and childhood within the structure of the family. My notions of relativity have more to do with establishing the boundary conditions for various analytic concepts, determining their relative importance within the edifice of psychoanalytic thought and separating what is Western-cultural in psychoanalytic formulations from what is truly universal. Very few theorists have engaged in this kind of thoughtful consideration of the cultural guises, disguises, elaborations and transformations of analytic concepts. Erikson, again, is a notable exception; for instance, when he summarizes (Erikson, 1979) the epistemological status of his theory of the life cycle thus:

While the exact *age* of onset and the *length* of any stage of development as well as the *intensity* of the conflict may all vary dramatically from one culture to another and from one individual to another, the *order* and *sequence* of these stages remain fixed; for they are intrinsically related both to physiological stages and to the basic requirements of any social order (p. 26).

To a large extent, the reason why attempts at a relativizing of major analytic concepts have not been more widely undertaken lies in the nature of the drive psychology theory itself. In its most widely accepted version, structurally, culture enters the psyche at a relatively late stage of development with the formation of the superego. Freud, though, attributed to an individual's social and cultural environment a more prominent role in the understanding of the superego than what might appear from reading most clinical reports today. In speaking of the manifestation and properties of the superego, Freud (1930) writes, 'We come across the remarkable circumstance that the mental processes concerned are actually more familiar to us and more accessible to consciousness as they are seen in the group than they can be in the individual man' (p. 142).

Besides the dismissal implicit in its characterization as 'later', as opposed to 'early', culture in the classical theory also suffers from the label of a 'surface' phenomenon and hence being 'superficial', rather than constituting a part of the 'depth' and hence being more 'fundamental' in the individual's psychic life. For, dynamically, the psychic depths of the repressed unconscious in the drive psychology model consist of the derivatives of phylogenetically determined sexual and aggressive impulse which are independent of the individual's cultural heritage. It is only in the more 'relational' theories, where the unconscious consists of particular images of the self and others which have been deemed unacceptable within the structure of the individual's society, that culture has an opportunity of appearing in the 'depths'.

An adherence to the classical drive theory is perhaps also the reason why psychoanalytic movements in the two non-Western societies, India and Japan, have failed to produce enough clinical material which could contribute to a highlighting of the cultural relativity of analytic concepts. Such an endeavour is not simply a matter of testing analytic postulates against available clinical data from these cultures. The separation of data from theory is an extremely difficult if not impossible task since it is our framework of ordering concepts that shapes our observations and explanations. As Greenberg and Mitchell (1983) have pointed out, the way a psychoanalyst views a patient and describes his conflicts, and the diagnostic categories he uses, are themselves contingent upon his theoretical propositions. The kind of cultural data I am talking about, which should normally be expected from the analyses of Indian and Japanese patients, is inevitably missing from reports of psychoanalytic observers who have a prior commitment to a theoretical model which excludes precisely such data as 'sociological' rather than 'psychological'.

The 'free floating attention' of the analyst, then, does not float quite as free as one may ideally suppose. It is weighed down by the analyst's theoretical predilections which fasten on some items in the patient's productions more than others. It is also bounded by his preconscious assumptions about nature, man and society, which, to a large extent, are culturally constituted. Normally, within the same society, these traditional propositions are the building blocks of a socially constructed reality shared by the patient, the analyst and the community of which they both form a part and thus remain a non-intrusive backdrop against which analytic work is carried out. A major problem in the practice of psychoanalysis in non-Western cultures (and in dynamic psychotherapy with patients from radically different ethnic groups in Western societies), however, is that the backdrop is not quite so neutral and, in fact, becomes an active intruder into the analytical process. The socially created and shared reality of non-Western patients is strikingly different in crucial respects from the analyst's own consciously chosen psychoanalytic world-view which has deep roots in the Western Zeitgeist of a particular historical period. Let me elaborate on this issue with reference to psychoanalysis in India.

The theoretical perspective of classical psychoanalysis is informed by a specific vision of human experience which emphasizes man's individuality and his self-contained, encapsulated, subjective world. This view of man, with a long history in Western political and social philosophy, became dominant during the period of Enlightenment. Together with other values of Enlightenment such as the existence and knowableness of an objective reality, the possibility of real choice, and what Kohut (1982) calls 'knowledge values and independence values of Western man', the individualist model of man has pervaded the fundamental premises of the classical drive psychology model. These premises, as Greenberg and Mitchell (1983) describe them, are:

1. The unit of study of psychoanalysis is the individual, viewed as a discrete entity. Man is not, in Aristotle's terms, a 'political animal'; he does not require a social organization to allow him to realize his true human potential. Society is imposed on an already complete individual for his protection, but at the cost of renunciation of many of his most important personal goals. It is thus possible and even necessary to speak of a person divorced from his interpersonal context . . .

2. The origin of every human activity can be traced ultimately to the demands of a drive . . . From the perspective of content the drives are reducible to two independent sets of needs which arise on the basis of man's biological inheritance. Their origin is in no way influenced by social context, and they stand in relation to society exactly as do Locke's 'natural rights' of life, liberty and property . . .

3. There is no inherent object, no preordained tie to the human environment. The object is 'created' by the individual out of the experience of drive satisfaction and frustration . . . (p. 44).

The view of the person based on these premises, Freud's version of the Enlightenment man, which directs the analyst's perceptions and actions in the analytic situation, cannot be held to be universally valid in all cultures and at all historical periods.

The Hindu view of the person, for instance, which comprises cultural propositions by means of which most people think about the nature of man in traditional India, holds the person to be 'dividual', i.e. divisible (Marriott, 1980). He is not a monad but (at least) dyadic, deriving his personal nature interpersonally. Individuality is not given at birth but is an achievement of the final stage of the life cycle when the person ideally becomes a 'renouncer' and succeeds in detaching himself from his human ties and relationships. Hindu persons, then, in the dominant image of their culture are constituted of relationships; all affects, needs and motives are relational and their distresses are disorders of relationships—not only of relationship with their human but also with their natural and cosmic orders. This emphasis on the dividual, trans-personal nature of man pervades Indian medical, astrological, anthropological and psychological theories and, to give an example, is strikingly illustrated in the cultural image of the body.

The Indian image of the body emphasizes its intimate connection with nature and the cosmos. As a nineteenth-century popular Bengali text (Chattopadhyaya, 1878) on the body puts it:

In this universe a great wheel of transformative power is spinning ceaselessly. The small individual wheels of transformative power in the bodies of living things are connected with that wheel. Just as, when some great steam-driven wheel turns like the prime mover, then all of the components of the machinery move together in co-ordination and smoothly accomplish their tasks, similarly the small wheels of transformative power than turn through their connection with that great wheel, within the bodies of individual living things, help accomplish such bodily activities as regulating the flow of blood in the body, digesting food, inhaling and exhaling, and moving back and forth (p. 31).

The Indian body image stresses an unremitting interchange taking place with the environment. In traditional medicine, Ayurveda, there is no map or topography of the body but only an *economy*, that is to say fluids going in or coming out, residing in some *asrya* (recipient) or flowing through some channels (Zimmermann, 1979). This is in sharp contrast to the Western individualistic image of a clearly etched body, sharply differentiated from the rest of the objects in the universe. Such a vision of the body as a safe stronghold with a limited number of drawbridges that maintain a tenuous contact with the outside world also underlies classical psychoanalytic theory. The location of the self and its processes, whether it is 'inside' the body or whether it expands outside the boundaries of the skin, is correspondingly different in the two orientations.

Even with the urbanized and highly literate individuals who form the bulk of clientele for psychoanalysis in India, the relational orientation is still the 'natural' way of viewing the self and the world. Thus it is not uncommon for family members, who often (and significantly!) accompany the patient for a first interview, to complain about the patient's *autonomy* as one of the symptoms of his disorder. Thus the father and elder sister of a 28-year-old engineer who had had a psychotic episode described their understanding of his chief problem as one of unnatural autonomy: 'He is very stubborn in pursuing what he wants, without taking our wishes into account. He thinks he knows what is best for him and does not listen to us. He thinks his own life and career are more important than the concerns of the rest of the family.'

I am, of course, not advancing any simplified dichotomy between a Western cultural image of an individual, autonomous self and a relational, transpersonal self of Indian and many other non-Western societies. Both visions of human experience are present in all the major cultures though a particular culture may, over a length of time, highlight and emphasize one at the expense of the other. Historically, man as a social animal has also been an important value in the Western tradition, though it may have been submerged at certain periods of history, especially in the nineteenth and early twentieth century. This, a so-called value of counter-Enlightenment (Berlin, 1979), is a part of the relativist and sceptical tradition that goes back to Western antiquity. It stresses that belonging to a community is a fundamental need of man and asserts that only if a man truly belongs to such a community, naturally and unselfconsciously, can he enter into the living stream and lead a full, creative spontaneous life. The counter-Enlightenment values have found renewed expression in the burgeoning number of adherents of the various relational models within psychoanalysis.

Whatever their relationship to drive psychology, these models—the names of Mahler, Winnicott, Kernberg, Kohut, Erikson, come immediately to mind—are in general agreement that the mental representations of relationships with others constitute the fundamental building blocks of mental life. The increasing importance of the 'relational' approaches in recent years, I would suggest, is not only due to changes in the kind of psychopathology seen among analytic patients but due to the receding of classical neuroses in favour of identity problems, borderline and narcissistic disorders, which have more to do with the absence and loss of objects in general and with which people are confronted today. The greater receptivity to these models and to their particular insights into human existence is perhaps also due to a re-assertion and renaissance of the values of counter-Enlightenment in Western societies, especially since the 1960s.

It is my contention that the relational models, with their different understanding of human development, psychoanalytic technique and therapeutic action, are congruent with the dominant cultural orientation and experience of people living in non-Western societies. The confinement of psychoanalysis to Western societies during the last eighty years and its stagnation (when it has ventured forth across their borders) in India and Japan over decades may well be due to the individualistic premises of the drive psychology model which clash with the dominant cultural orientation of non-Western societies. Psychoanalysis perhaps does not and cannot overthrow the fundamental cultural propositions about the nature of man, human experience and the fulfilled human life. What it can uniquely do is to give these premises specific analytic content: a dynamic view in which life is determined by a complex interplay of motivational forces that are often in conflict, which function outside our normal awareness, and which can be brought to consciousness in the kind of intense collaborative inquiry that is the hallmark of the psychoanalytic situation.

Summary

Problems in psychoanalytic writings on non-Western cultures, such as questionable yardsticks of evaluation, the incorporation of Western middle-class experience and values into some of the analytic concepts which are then considered as universally valid, are discussed with examples from clinical practice in India. It is suggested that the confinement of psychoanalysis to the West and its relative stagnation in the two non-Western societies of India and Japan may well have to do with the model of man underlying classical drive psychology. The very nature of the drive psychology model excludes a consideration of cultural data and thus hinders any relativizing of analytic concepts. The dominant concept of man in most non-Western societies is more relational than individual. The newer relational theories in psychoanalysis may therefore find a greater resonance and better reception in non-Western cultures than the traditional psychoanalytic version of Enlightenment man.

REFERENCES

Berlin, I. (1979), 'The Counter-Enlightenment', in *Against the Current: Essays in the History of Ideas*, London: Hogarth Press.

Boyer, L. G. (1962), 'Remarks on the Personality of Shamans: with Special Reference to the Apache of the Mescalero Indian Reservation', *Psychoanal. Study Society*, 2: 233–54.

Chattopadhyaya, K. D. (1878), *The Doctrine of the Body*, tr. A. A. Sarkar, Department of Anthropology, Univ. of Chicago.

Daly, C. D. (1927), 'Hindu-Mythologie und Kastrations-Komplex', *American Imago*, 13: 145–98.

Devereux, G. (1956), 'Normal and Abnormal', in *Basic Problems in Ethnopsychiatry*, Chicago: Univ. of Chicago Press, 1980.

Erikson, E. H. (1963), *Childhood and Society*, New York: Norton.

——— (1979), 'Report to Vikram: further Perspectives on the Life Cycle', in S. Kakar ed., *Identity and Adulthood*, Delhi: Oxford Univ. Press.

Freud, S. (1912), 'Recommendations to Physicians Practising Psychoanalysis', *S.E.* 12.

——— (1939), 'Civilization and its Discontents', *S.E.* 21.

Greenberg, J. R. and Mitchell, S. A. (1983), *Object Relations in Psychoanalytic Theory*. Cambridge, Mass: Harvard Univ. Press.

Kakar, S. (1978), *The Inner World: A Psychoanalytic Study of Childhood and Society in India*, New York and Delhi: Oxford Univ. Press.

——— (1982), *Shamans, Mystics and Doctors*, New York: Alfred Knopf.

Kohut, H. (1982), 'Introspection, Empathy and the Semi-circle of Mental Health', *Int. Journal of Psychoanalysis*, 63: 395–407.

Marriott, M. (1980), 'The Open Hindu Person and Interpersonal Fluidity', unpublished paper read at Association for Asian Studies Meetings, Washington, D.C.

Masson, J. M. (1980), *The Oceanic Feeling*, Dordrecht: Reidel.

Mitchell, J. D. (1957), 'The Sanskrit Drama Shakuntala and the Oedipus Complex', *American Imago*, 14: 389–405.

Roheim, G. (1945), *Eternal Ones of the Dream: A Psychoanalytic Interpretation of Australian Myth and Ritual*, New York: Int. Univ. Press.

—— (1950), *Psychoanalysis and Anthropology: Culture Personality and the Unconscious*, New York: Int. Univ. Press.

Roland, A. (1980), 'Psychoanalytic Perspectives on Personality Development in India', *Int. Rev. of Psychoanalysis*, 7: 73–87.

Silvan, M. (1981), Reply to Allan Roland's paper on 'Psychoanalytic Perspectives on Personality Development in India', *Int. Rev. of Psychoanalysis*, 8: 93–9.

Simon, B. and Weiner, H. (1966), 'Models of Mind and Mental Illness in Ancient Greece', *Journal History of Behavioral Sciences*, 2: 303–14.

Sinha, T. C. (1977), 'Psychoanalysis and the Family in India', *Samiksa*, 31: 95–105.

Zimmerman, F. (1979), 'Remarks on the Conception of the Body in Ayurvedic Medicine'. Paper presented at the ACLS-SSRC Seminar on the person and interpersonal relations in South Asia. Univ. of Chicago.

5

Clinical Work
and Cultural Imagination

The perennial question of the cross-cultural validity of psychoanalysis actually has two parts: Is psychoanalysis at all possible in a traditional non-Western society with its different family system, religious beliefs and cultural values? Is the mental life of non-Western patients radically different from that of their Western counterparts?

Over the years, in my own talks to diverse audiences in Europe and the United States, the question of trans-cultural validity of psychoanalysis has invariably constituted the core of animated discussion. The sharp increase in scepticism about this particular question has in recent years been correlated with the rise of relativism in the human sciences. Intellectually, the relativistic position owes much of its impetus to Foucault's powerful argument on the rootedness of all thought in history and culture—and in the framework of power relations. Adherents of this perspective are not a priori willing to accept why psychoanalysis, a product of nineteenth-century European bourgeois family and social structure, should be an exception to the general rule of the incapacity of thought to transcend its roots. In this paper, I propose to discuss the issue of the cultural rootedness of psychoanalysis with illustrations from my own clinical practice in India.

Ramnath was a 51-year-old man who owned a grocery shop in the oldest part of the city of Delhi. When he came to see me some eighteen years ago, he was suffering from a number of complaints, though he desired my help for only one of them—an unspecified 'fearfulness'. This anxiety, less than three years old, was a relatively new development. His migraine headaches, on the other hand went back to his adolescence. Ramnath attributed them to an excess of 'wind' in the stomach, which periodically

First published in *Psychoanalytic Quarterly*, 64, 1995. Reprinted with permission.

rose up and pressed against the veins in his head. Ramnath had always had a nervous stomach. It is now never quite as bad as it was in the months following his marriage some thirty years ago, when it was accompanied by severe stomach cramps and an alarming weight loss. He was first taken to the hospital by his father, where he was X-rayed and tested. Finding nothing wrong with him, the doctors had prescribed a variety of vitamins and tonics which were not of much help. Older family members and friends had then recommended a nearby *ojha*—'sorcerer' is too fierce a translation for this mild-mannered professional of ritual exorcism—who diagnosed his condition as the result of magic practised by an enemy, namely, his newly acquired father-in-law. The rituals to counteract the enemy magic were expensive, as was the yellowish liquid emetic prescribed by the *ojha*, which periodically forced Ramnath to empty his stomach with gasping heaves. In any event, he was fully cured within two months of the *ojha*'s treatment, and the cramps and weight loss have not recurred.

Before coming to see me about his 'fearfulness', Ramnath had been treated with drugs by various doctors: by allopaths (as Western-style doctors are called in India) as well as homeopaths, by the *vaids* of Hindu medicine as well as the *hakims* of the Islamic medical tradition. He had consulted psychiatrists, ingested psychotropic drugs, and submitted to therapy. He had gone through the rituals of two *ojhas* and was thinking of consulting a third who was highly recommended.

His only relief came through the weekly gathering of the local chapter of the Brahmakumari (literally 'Virgins of Brahma') sect which he had recently joined. The communal meditations and singing gave him a feeling of temporary peace and his nights were no longer so restless. Ramnath was puzzled by the persistence of his anxious state and its various symptoms. He had tried to be a good man, he said, according to his *dharma*, which is both the 'right conduct' of his caste and the limits imposed by his own character and predispositions. He had worshipped the gods and attended services in the temple with regularity, even contributing generously toward the consecration of a Krishna idol in his native village in Rajasthan. He did not have any bad habits, he asserted. Tea and cigarettes, yes, but for a couple of years he had abjured even these minor though pleasurable addictions. Yet the anxiety persisted, unremitting and unrelenting.

Since it is culture rather than psyche which is the focus of this presentation, let me essay a cultural—rather than a psycho—analysis of Ramnath's condition. At first glance, Ramnath's cognitive space in matters of illness and well-being seems incredibly cluttered. Gods and spirits, community and family, food and drink, personal habits and character, all seem to be somehow intimately involved in the maintenance of health. Yet these and other factors such as biological infection, social pollution, and cosmic displeasure, all of which most Hindus would also acknowledge as causes of ill health—only point to the recognition of a person's simultaneous existence in different orders of being; of the person being a body, a psyche and a social being at the same time. Ramnath's experience of his illness may appear alien to Europeans only because, as I have elaborated elsewhere (Kakar, 1982), the body, the psyche, and the community do not possess fixed, immutable meanings across cultures. The concept of the body and the understanding of its processes are not quite the same in India as they are in the West. The Hindu body, portrayed in relevant cultural texts, predominantly in imagery from the vegetable kingdom, is much more intimately connected with the cosmos than the clearly etched Western body which is sharply differentiated from the rest of the objects in the universe. The Hindu body image stresses an unremitting interchange taking place with the environment, simultaneously accompanied by ceaseless change within the body. The psyche—the Hindu 'subtle body'—is not primarily a psychological category in India. It is closer to the ancient Greek meaning of the 'psyche', the source of all vital activities and psychic processes, and considered capable of persisting in its disembodied state after death. Similarly, for many Indians, the community consists not only of living members of the family and the social group but also of ancestral and other spirits as well as the gods and goddesses who populate the Hindu cosmos. An Indian is inclined to believe that his or her illness can reflect a disturbance in any one of these orders of being, while the symptoms may also be manifested in the other orders. If a treatment, say, in the bodily order fails, one is quite prepared to reassign the cause of the illness to a different order and undergo its particular curing regimen—prayers or exorcisms, for instance—without losing regard for other methods of treatment.

The involvement of all orders of being in health and illness means that an Indian is generally inclined to seek more than one cause for illness in especially intractable cases. An Indian tends to view these causes as complementary rather than exclusive and arranges them in a hierarchical order by identifying an immediate cause as well as others that are more remote. The causes are arranged in concentric circles, with the outer circle including all the inner ones.

To continue with our example: Ramnath had suffered migraine head-aches since his adolescence. Doctors of traditional Hindu medicine, Ayurveda, had diagnosed the cause as a humoral disequilibrium—an excess of 'wind' in the stomach which periodically rose up and pressed against the veins in his head—and prescribed Ayurbedic drugs, dietary restrictions as well as liberal doses of aspirin. Such a disequilibrium is usually felt to be compounded by bad habits which, in turn, demand changes in personal conduct. When an illness like Ramnath's persists, its stubborn intensity will be linked with his unfavourable astrological conditions, requiring palliative measures such as a round of prayers (*puja*). The astrological 'fault' probably will be further traced back to the bad karma of a previous birth about which, finally, nothing can be done—except, perhaps, the cultivation of a stoic endurance with the help of the weekly meetings of the Virgins of Brahma sect.

I saw Ramnath thrice a week in psychoanalytic therapy for twenty-one sessions before he decided to terminate the treatment. At the time, although acutely aware of my deficiencies as a novice, I had placed the blame for the failure of the therapy on the patient or, to be more exact, on the cultural factors involved in his decision. Some of these were obvious. Ramnath had slotted me into a place normally reserved for a personal guru. From the beginning, he envisioned not a contractual doctor–patient relationship but a much more intimate guru–disciple bond that would allow him to abdicate responsibility for his life. He was increasingly dismayed that a psychoanalyst did not dispense wise counsel but expected the client to talk, that I wanted to follow his lead rather than impose my own views or directions on the course of our sessions. My behaviour also went against the guru model which demands that the therapist demonstrate his compassion, interest, warmth and responsiveness much more openly than I believed is possible or desirable in a psychoanalytic relationship. I did not know then that Ramnath's 'guru fantasy', namely the existence of someone, somewhere—now discovered in my person—who will heal the wounds suffered in all past relationships, remove the blights on the soul so that it shines anew in its pristine state, was not inherent in his Indianness but common across many cultures. Irrespective of their conscious subscription to the ideology of egalitarianism and a more contractual doctor–patient relationship, my

European and American patients too approached analysis and the analyst with a full blown guru fantasy which, though, was more hidden and less accessible to consciousness than in the case of Ramnath.

More than Ramnath's expectations, it was the disappointment of mine, I now realize, on which the analysis floundered. I had expected Ramnath to be an individual in the sense of someone whose consciousness has been moulded in a crucible which is commonly regarded as having come into existence as part of the psychological revolution in the wake of the Enlightenment in Europe. This revolution, of course, is supposed to have narrowed the older, metaphysical scope of the mind, to mind as an isolated island of individual consciousness, profoundly aware of its almost limitless subjectivity and its infantile tendency to heedless projection and illusion. Psychoanalysis, I believed, with some justification, is possible only with a person who is individual in this special sense, who shares, at some level of awareness and to some minimum degree, the modern vision of human experience wherein each of us lives in his own subjective world, pursuing personal pleasures and private fantasies, constructing a fate which will vanish when our time is over. The reason why in most psychoanalytic case histories, whether in Western or non-Western worlds, analysands, except for their different neurotic or character disturbances, sound pretty much like each other (and like their analysts), is because they all share the post-Enlightenment world-view of what constitutes an individual. In a fundamental sense, psychoanalysis does not have a cross-cultural context but takes place in the same culture across different societies; it works in the established (and expanding) enclaves of psychological modernity around the world. We can therefore better understand why psychoanalysis in India began in Calcutta— the first capital of the British empire in India where Indians began their engagement and confrontation with post-Enlightenment Western thought— before extending itself and virtually limiting itself to Bombay which prides itself on its cosmopolitan character and cultural 'modernity'. It is also comprehensible that the clientele for psychoanalysis in India consists overwhelmingly—though not completely—of individuals (and their family members) who are involved in modern professions like journalism, advertising, academia, law, medicine and so on. In its sociological profile, at least, this clientele does not significantly differ from one that seeks psychoanalytic therapy in Europe and America.

Ramnath, I believed, was not an individual in the sense that he lacked 'psychologically modernity'. He had manfully tried to understand the psychoanalytic model of inner conflict rooted in life history that was implied in my occasional interventions. It was clear that this went against his cultural model of psychic distress and healing wherein the causes for his suffering lay outside himself and had little to do with his biography—black magic by father-in-law, disturbed planetary constellations, bad karma from previous life, disturbed humoral equilibrium. He was thus not suitable for psychoanalytic therapy and perhaps I had given up on him before he gave up on me. But Ramnath, I realized later, like many of my other traditional Hindu patients, had an individuality which is embedded in and expressed in terms from the Hindu cultural universe. This individuality is accessible to psychoanalysis if the therapist is willing and able to build the required bridges from a modern to a traditional individuality. The Indian analyst has to be prepared, for instance, to interpret the current problems of such a patient in terms of his or her bad karma—feelings, thoughts and actions—not from a previous existence but from a forgotten life, the period of infancy and childhood, his or her 'pre-history'. Let me elaborate on this distinction between traditional and modern individuals who both share what I believe is the essence of psychological modernity.

Psychological modernity, although strongly associated with post-Enlightenment, is nevertheless not identical with it. The core of psychological modernity is internalization rather than externalization. I use internalization here as a sensing by the person of a psyche in the Greek sense, an animation from within rather than without. Experientially, this internalization is a recognition that one is possessed of a mind in all its complexity. It is the acknowledgement, however vague, unwilling or conflicted, of a subjectivity that fates one to episodic suffering through some of its ideas and feelings—in psychoanalysis, murderous rage, envy, and possessive desire seeking to destroy those one loves and would keep alive—simultaneously with the knowledge, at some level of awareness, that the mind can help in containing and processing disturbed thoughts—as indeed can the family and the group as well (Bollas, 1992). In Hindu terms, it is a person's sense and acknowledgement of the primacy of the 'subtle body'—the *sukshmasharira*—in human action and of human suffering as caused by the workings of the five passions: sexual desire, rage, greed, infatuation and egotism. Similarly, Buddhists too describe human suffering as being due to causes internal to the individual: cognitive factors such as a perceptual cloudiness causing mis-perception of objects of awareness but also affective causes such as agitation and worry—the elements of anxiety, and greed, avarice and envy which form the cluster of grasping attachment. This *internalization* is the essence of 'individuation', and of psychological modernity, which has always been a part of what Hindus call the 'more evolved' beings in traditional civilizations. The fact that this core of individuation is expressed in a religious rather than a psychological idiom should not prevent us from recognizing its importance as an ideal of maturity in traditional civilizations such as Hindu India; it should also give us pause in characterizing, indeed with the danger of pathologizing India or any other civilization as one where some kind of familial self (Roland, 1990) or group mind (Kurtz, 1992) reigns in individual mental life. The 'evolved' Hindu in the past or even in the present who has little to do with the post-Enlightenment West, thus interprets the *Mahabharata* as an account of inner conflict in man's soul rather than of outer hostilities. The 'evolved beings' in India, including the most respected gurus, have always held that the guru, too, is only seemingly a person but actually a function, a transitional object in modern parlance, as are all the various gods who, too, are only aspects of the self. 'The Guru is the disciple, but perfected, complete,' says Muktananda (1983). 'When he forms a relationship with the guru, the disciple is in fact forming a relationship with his own best self' (p. ix). At the end of your *sadhana*, burn the guru, say the tantriks; kill the Buddha if you meet him on the way, is a familiar piece of Zen Buddhist wisdom. All of them, gurus or gods (as also the analyst), have served the purpose of internalization—of a specific mode of relating to and experiencing the self, and are dispensable.

Psychological modernity is thus not coterminous with historical modernity, nor are its origins in a specific geographical location even if it received a sharp impetus from the European Enlightenment. My biggest error in Ramnath's case was in making a sharp dichotomy between a 'Hindu' cultural view of the interpersonal and transpersonal nature of man and a modern 'Western' view of man's individual and instinctual nature and assuming that since Ramnath was not an individual in the latter sense, he was not an individual at all. Although suggestive and fruitful for cultural understanding, the individual/relational differences should not be overemphasized. Even my distinction between traditional and modern individuality is not a sharp one. In reference to his satori or enlightenment, occasioned by the cry of a crow, Ikkyu, a fifteenth-century Zen master, known for his colourful eccentricity, suggests the presence of a 'modern' biographical individuality when he writes:

ten dumb years I wanted things to be different furious proud I
still feel it
one summer night in my little boat on lake Biwa
caaaawwweeeee
father when I was a boy you left us now I forgive you (Berg, 1989, p. 42).

In spite of the cultural highlighting of the inter- and transpersonal I found my traditional Indian patients more individual in their unconscious than they initially realized. Similarly, in spite of a Western cultural emphasis on autonomous individuality, my European and American patients are more relational than *they* realize. Individual and communal, self and other, are complementary ways of looking at the organization of mental life and exist in a dialectical relationship to each other although a culture may, over a period of time, stress the importance of one or the other in its ideology of the fulfilled human life and thus shape a person's *conscious* experience of the self in predominantly individual or communal modes. It is undeniable that Indians are very relational, with the family and community (including the family of divinities) playing a dominant role in the experience of the self. It is also undeniable, though less evident, that Indians are very individualistic and, at least in fantasy, are capable of conceiving and desiring a self free of *all* attachments and relationships.

In positing some shared fundamentals for the practice of the psychoanalytic enterprise, I do not mean to imply that there is no difference between analysands from Bombay, Beirut or Birmingham. The middle-class, educated, urban Indian although more individualized in his experience of the self and closer to his Western counterpart on this dimension, is nevertheless not identical with the latter. Contrary to the stance popular among many anthropologists of Indian society, the traditional Hindu villager is not the only Indian there is with the rest being some kind of imposters or cultural deviants. The urban Indian analysand shares with others many of the broader social and cultural patterns which are reflected in the cultural particularities of the self. One of these particularities, frequently met with in case histories and a dominant motif in Hindu myths and other products of cultural imagination, is the centrality of the male Hindu Indian's experience of the powerful mother (Kakar, 1978; 1990). Let me first illustrate this more concretely through a vignette.

Pran, a thirty-five year old journalist, came to analysis suffering from a general, unspecified anxiety and what he called a persistent feeling of being always on the 'edge'. Until March of that year, Pran's 320 sessions have been pervaded by his mother to a degree unsurpassed in my clinical work. For almost two years, four times a week, hour after hour, Pran would recollect what his mother told him on this or that particular occasion, what she thought, believed or said, as he struggles to dislodge her from the throne on which he has ensconced her in the deepest recesses of his psyche. She was a deeply religious woman, a frequenter of discourses given by various holy men, to which Pran accompanied her and which contributed significantly to the formation of his traditional Hindu world view. In contrast to the mother, Pran's memories of his father, who died when he was eleven, are scant. They are also tinged with a regret that Pran did not get a chance to be closer to a figure who remains dim and was banished to the outskirts of family life when alive. He is clearly and irrevocably dead while the mother, who died ten years ago, is very much alive. The father was a man about town, rarely at home, and thoroughly disapproved of by the mother who not only considered herself more virtuous and intelligent, but also implied to the son that the stroke which finally killed his father was a consequence of his dissolute, 'manly' ways.

Pran's memories of his closeness to his mother, the hours they spent just sitting together, communing in silence, a feeling of deep repose flowing through him, are many. He remembers being breast fed till he was eight or nine, although when he thinks about it a little more, he doubts whether there was any milk in the breasts for many of those years. In any event, he distinctly recollects peremptorily lifting up her blouse whenever he felt like a suck, even when she was busy talking to other women. Her visiting friends were at times indulgent and at other indignant, 'Why don't you stop him?' they would ask his mother. 'He does not listen,' she would reply in mock helplessness.

Pran slept in his mother's bed till he was eighteen. He vividly recalls the peculiar mixture of dread and excitement, especially during the adolescence years, when he would manoeuvre his erect penis near her vagina for that most elusive and forbidden of touches which he was never sure was a touch at all, where he never knew whether his penis had actually been in contact with her body. Later, his few physical encounters with women were limited to hugging, while he awkwardly contorted the lower part of his body to keep his erection beyond their ken. For a long time, his sexual fantasies were limited to looking at and touching a woman's breasts. As his analysis progressed, his most pleasurable sexual fantasy became one of the penis hovering on the brink of the labial lips, even briefly touching them, but never of entering the woman's body.

After his studies, at which he was very good, Pran joined a newspaper and became quite successful. The time for his marriage had now arrived and there began the first open though still subdued conflicts with his mother on the choice of a marriage partner. His mother invariably reject-ed every attractive woman he fancied, stating bluntly that sons forget their mothers if they get into the clutches of a beautiful woman. Pran finally agreed to his mother's choice of a docile and plain-looking woman. For the first six months, he felt no desire for his wife. (The fact that his mother slept in the room next to the bridal couple and insisted that the connecting door remain open at all times except for the hours of the night, did not exactly work as an aphrodisiac.) When the family used the car, the wife would sit at the back, the mother not holding with new-fangled modern notions which would relegate her to the back seat once the son had brought a wife home. Even now his sexual desire for his wife is perfunctory and occasional. He feels excited by women with short hair who wear make-up and skirts rather than an long-tressed Indian beauty in the traditional attire of *salwar kameez* or *sari*. Such a woman is too near the mother. For many years, Pran has been trying to change his wife's conservative appearance, so reminiscent of the mother's, to-ward one which is closer to the object of his desire.

It was only after his mother's death that Pran experienced sexual inter-course with his wife as pleasurable. Yet after intercourse there is invariably a feeling of tiredness for a couple of days and Pran feels, as he puts it, that his body is 'breaking'. His need for food, especially the spicy-sour savour-ies (*chat*) which were a special favourite of the mother and are popularly considered 'woman's food', goes up markedly. In spite of his tiredness, Pran can drive miles in search of the spicy fare.

The need for sleep and spicy food, together with the feeling of physical unease, also occurs at certain other times. A regular feature of his work day is that after a few hours of work, he feels the need for something to eat and a short nap. The physical unease, the craving for food and sleep increase dramatically when he has to travel on business or to take people out for dinner. It is particularly marked if he ever has a drink at a bar with friends.

Relatively early in his analysis, Pran became aware of the underlying pattern in his behaviour. Going to work, travelling, drinking and, of course, sexual intercourse, are 'manly' activities to which he is greatly drawn. They are, however, also experienced as a separation from the mother which give rise to anxiety till he must come back to her, for food and sleep. He must recurrently merge with her in order, as he put it, to strengthen his nervous system. The re-establishment of an oral connection with the mother is striking in its details. Pran not only hankers after the mother's favourite foods but feels a great increase in the sensitivity of the lips and the palate. The texture and taste of food in the mouth is vastly more important for the process of his recuperation than is the food's function in filling his belly. His sensual memories of his mother's breasts and the taste of her nipples in the mouth are utterly precise. He can recover the body of the early mother as a series of spaced flashes, as islands of memory. The short naps he takes after one of his 'manly' activities are framed in a special ritual. He lies down on his stomach with his face burrowed between two soft pillows, fantasizes about hugging a woman before he falls asleep, and wakes up fresh and vigorous.

It took longer time for Pran to become aware of the terror his mother's overwhelming invasiveness inspired in the little boy and his helpless rage in dealing with it. He railed, and continues to do so, at her selfishness which kept him bound to her and wept at memories of countless occasions when she would ridicule his efforts to break away from her in play with other boys, or in the choice of his workplace, clothes, or friends. She has destroyed his masculinity, he feels. As a boy, she made him wash her underclothes, squeeze out the discharge from her nipples, oil her hair and pluck out the grey ones on an almost daily basis. The birth of his four daughters, he felt, was due to this feminization which had made his semen 'weak'. He realized that all his 'manly' activities were not only in pursuit of individuation as a man, or even in a quest for pleasure but also because they would lacerate the mother. 'I always wanted to hurt her and at the same time I could not do without her. She has been raping me ever since I was born,' he once said.

Often, as he lies there, abusing the mother, with a blissful expression on his face reflecting her close presence, I cannot help but feel that this is *nindastuti*, worship of a divinity through insult, denigration and contempt, which is one of the recognized relationships of a Hindu devotee with a divinity.

I have selected this particular vignette from my case histories because in its palette of stark, primary colours and in its lack of complex forms and subtle shades, it highlights, even caricatures, a dominant theme in the analysis of many male Hindu Indians. Judged by its frequency of occurrence in clinical work and in its pre-eminence in the Hindu cultural imagination, the theme of what I call maternal enthrallment and the issue of the boy's separation from the overwhelming maternal—feminine—rather than the dilemmas of Oedipus—appears to be the hegemonic (to use the fashionable Gramscian term) narrative of the Hindu family drama (Kakar, 1989). It is the cornerstone in the architecture of the male self. The reason why I mention cultural imagination in conjunction with clinical work when advancing a generalized psychoanalytic proposition about the Indian cultural context, is simple. Clinical psychoanalysis is generally limited to a small sample from three or four large Indian metro-polises. It cannot adequately take into account the heterogeneity of a country of eight hundred million people with its regional, linguistic, religious and caste divisions. Clinical cases can, at best, generate hypotheses about cultural particularities. The further testing of these hypotheses is done (and remains true to psychoanalytic intention and enterprise) by testing them in the crucible of the culture's imagination.

The kind of maternal enthrallment and the prolonged mother–son symbiosis I have described in this particular vignette, including the peek-a-boo, was-it-or-was-it-not incest, would ordinarily be associated with much greater pathology in analytic case conferences in Europe and North America. Pran's level of functioning, however, is quite impressive in spite of his many inhibitions and anxieties, especially sexual. I wonder how much of this kind of psychoanalytical expectation that Pran is sicker than what I believe to be actually the case, is due to a cultural contamination creeping into the clinical judgement of his sexual differentiation and separation–individuation processes. For instance, is the psychoanalytic evaluation of Pran's undoubted feminization and a certain lack of differentiation also being influenced by a Western cultural imagination on what it means to be, look, think and behave like a man or a woman? This becomes clearer if one thinks of Greek or Roman sculpture with their hard, muscled men's bodies and chests without any fat at all and compares it with the sculpted representations of Hindu gods or the Buddha where the bodies are softer, suppler and, in their hint of breasts, nearer to the female form.

I have no intention of relativizing Pran's pain and suffering out of existence. I only wish to point out that between a minimum of sexual differentiation that is required to function heterosexually with a modicum of pleasure, and a maximum which cuts off any sense of empathy and emotional contact with the other sex which is then experienced as a different species altogether, there is a whole range of positions, each occupied by a culture which insists on calling it the only one that is mature and healthy.

Compared to a modal Western analysand, then (and one needs to postulate such a being if civilizational comparisons are to be made) his Hindu counterpart highlights different intra-psychic issues and places different accents on universal developmental experiences. Yet, perhaps because of an underlying similarity in the psychoanalytic clientele across cultures, discussed earlier, cultural otherness does not spring the psychoanalytic framework, made increasingly flexible by a profusion of models. Clinical work in India is thus not radically different from that in Europe and America. An analyst from outside the culture, encountering the strangeness of the cultural mask rather than the similarity of the individual face, may get carried away into exaggerating differences. However, if he could listen long enough and with a well-tuned ear for the analysand's symbolic and linguistic universes, he would discover that individual voices speaking of the whirling of imperious passion, the stabs of searing, burdensome guilt, the voracious hungers of the urge to merge, and the black despair at the absence of the Other, are as much evident here as in the psychoanalysis of Western patients.

Clinical work in another culture, however, does make us aware that because of the American and European domination of psychoanalytic discourse, Western cultural (and moral) imagination sometimes tends to slip into psychoanalytic theorizing as hidden 'health and maturity moralities', as Kohut (1979, p. 12) called them. Cultural judgements about psychological maturity, the nature of reality, 'positive' and 'negative' resolutions of conflicts and complexes often appear in the garb of psychoanalytic universals. Awareness of the cultural contexts of psychoanalysis would therefore contribute to increasing the ken and tolerance of our common discipline for the range of human variations and a much greater circumspection in dealing with notions of pathology and deviance.

Summary

Based on clinical experience with Hindu patients in India, this essay tries to address the question of the cross-cultural validity of psychoanalysis, namely whether psychoanalysis is possible with culturally traditional individuals in non-Western societies and if so, whether there is a radical difference in the mental life of these patients. A core requirement for psychoanalysis, it is argued, is the presence of psychological modernity, an awareness at some level in the individual that to a large extent both emotional suffering and its healing have their sources in what may be called a mind, which is internal to the individual. Psychological modernity, the essence of individuation and individuality, is not limited to any particular historical period or geographic location but is also found in traditional non-Western civilizations such as the Hindu or the Buddhist. Psychoanalysis is therefore eminently possible with persons who do not share the modern Western version of psychological modernity but subscribe instead to their own traditional concept of individuation. This does not mean that there are no differences at all between, say, European and Hindu patients. We find the mental life of the latter often highlighting themes—such as the theme of 'maternal enthrallment'—which, because of its different salience (as compared, for example, to the oedipal motif) in Western cultural imagination, may tend to be too easily or too quickly pathologized in Western analytical discourse.

REFERENCES

Berg, S. (1989), *Crow with No Mouth: Ikkyu-15th Century Zen Master*, Port Townsend: Copper Canyon Press.

Bollas, C. (1992), *Being a Character: Psychoanalysis and Self-experience*, New York: Hill and Wang.

Kakar, S. (1978), *The Inner World: A Psychoanalytic Study of Childhood and Society in India*, Delhi: Oxford Univ. Press.

—— (1982), *Shamans, Mystics and Doctors*, New York: Alfred Knopf.

—— (1989), 'The Maternal–feminine in Indian Psychoanalysis', *Int. Rev. of Psychoanalysis,* 16(3).

—— (1990), *Intimate Relations: Exploring Indian Sexuality*, Chicago: Univ. of Chicago Press.

Kohut, H. (1979), 'The Two Analyses of Mr Z', *Int. Journal of Psychoanalysis*, 60.

Kurtz, S. (1992), *All the Mothers are One: Hindu India and the Cultural Reshaping of Psychoanalysis*, New York: Columbia Univ. Press.

Muktananda, S. (1983), *The Perfect Relationship*, Ganeshpuri: Guru Siddha Vidyapeeth.

Roland, A. (1990), *In Search of Self in India and Japan*, Princeton: Princeton Univ. Press.

6

The Maternal–Feminine in Indian Psychoanalysis

On 11 April 1929, Girindrasekhar Bose, the founder and first president of the Indian Psychoanalytical Society, wrote to Freud on the difference he had observed in the psychoanalytic treatment of Indian and Western patients:

Of course I do not expect that you would accept offhand my reading of the Oedipus situation. I do not deny the importance of the castration threat in European cases; my argument is that the threat owes its efficiency to its connection with the wish to be female [Freud in a previous letter had gently chided Bose with understating the efficiency of the castration threat]. The real struggle lies between the desire to be a male and its opposite, the desire to be a female. I have already referred to the fact that castration threat is very common in Indian society but my Indian patients do not exhibit castration symptoms to such a marked degree as my European cases. The desire to be female is more easily unearthed in Indian male patients than in European . . . The Oedipus mother is very often a combined parental image and this is a fact of great importance. I have reason to believe that much of the motivation of the 'maternal deity' is traceable to this source.

Freud's reply is courteous and diplomatic: 'I am fully impressed by the difference in the castration reaction between Indian and European patients and promise to keep my attention fixed on the opposite wish you accentuate. The latter is too important for a hasty decision' (Sinha, 1966, p. 66).

In another paper, Bose (1950) elaborates on his observations and explains them through his theory of opposite wishes:

First published in *International Review of Psychoanalysis*, 16(3), 1989. Reprinted with the permission of the Institute of Psychoanalysis, London.

During my analysis of Indian patients I have never come across a case of castration complex in the form in which it has been described by European observers. This fact would seem to indicate that the castration idea develops as a result of environmental conditions acting on some more primitive trend in the subject. The difference in social environment of Indians and European is responsible for the difference in modes of expression in two cases. It has been usually proposed that threat of castration in early childhood days, owing to some misdemeanour, is directly responsible for the complex, but histories of Indian patients seem to disprove this (p. 74).

Bose then goes on to say that though the castration threat is extremely common—in girls it takes the form of chastisement by snakes—the difference in Indian reactions to it is due to children growing up naked till the ages of 9 to 10 years (girls till 7) so that the difference between the sexes never comes as a surprise. The castration idea which comes up symbolically in dreams as decapitation, a cut on a finger or a sore in some parts of the body has behind it the 'primitive' idea of being a woman.

Indeed, reading early Indian case histories, one is struck by the fluidity of the patients' cross-sexual and generational identifications. In the Indian patient the fantasy of taking on the sexual attributes of both the parents seems to have relatively easier access to awareness. Bose, for instance, in one of his vignettes (Bose, 1948) tells us of a middle-aged lawyer who, with reference to his parents, sometimes

took up an active male sexual role, treating both of them as females in his unconscious and sometimes a female attitude, especially towards the father, craving for a child from him. In the male role, sometimes he identified himself with his father and felt a sexual craving for the mother; on the other occasions his unconscious mind built up a composite of both the parents toward which male sexual needs were directed; it is in this attitude that he made his father give birth to a child like a woman in his dream (p. 158).

Another young Bengali (Bose, 1949), whenever he thought of a particular man, felt with a hallucinatory intensity that his penis and testes vanished altogether and were replaced by female genitalia. While defecating he felt he heard the peremptory voice of his guru asking, 'Have you given me a child yet?' In many of his dreams, he was a man whereas his father and brothers had become women. During intercourse with his wife he tied a handkerchief over his eyes as it gave him the feeling of being a veiled bride while he fantasized his own penis as that of his father and his wife's vagina as that of his mother.

In my own work, fifty years after Bose's contributions of which till recently I was only vaguely aware, I am struck by the comparable patterns in Indian mental life we observed independently of each other, and this in spite of our different emotional predilections, analytic styles, theoretical preoccupations, geographical locations and historical situations. Such a convergence further strengthens my belief, shared by every practising analyst, that there is no absolute arbitrariness in our representation of the inner world. There is unquestionably something that resists, a something which can only be characterized by the attribute 'psychical reality' which both the analyst and the analysand help discover and give meaning to.

It is the ubiquity and multiformity of the 'primitive idea of being a woman', and the embeddedness of this fantasy in the maternal configurations of the family and the culture in India, which I would like to discuss from my observations. My main argument is that the 'hegemonic narrative' of Hindu culture as far as male development is concerned is neither that of Freud's Oedipus nor that of Christianity's Adam. One of the more dominant narratives of this culture is that of Devi, the great goddess, especially in her manifold expressions as mother, in the inner world of the Hindu son. In India at least, a primary task of psychoanalysis, the science of imagination or even (in Wallace Stevens' words) 'the science of illusion'—*Mayalogy*—is to grapple with *Mahamaya*, 'The Great Illusion', as the goddess is also called. Of course, it is not my intention to deny or underestimate the importance of the powerful mother in Western psychoanalysis. All I seek to suggest is that certain forms of the maternal-feminine may be more central in Indian myths and psyche than in their western counterparts. I would then like to begin my exposition with the first ten minutes of an analytic session.

The patient is a 26-year-old social worker who has been in analysis for three years. He comes four times a week with each session lasting fifty minutes and conducted in the classical manner with the patient lying on the couch and the analyst sitting in a chair behind him. He entered analysis not because of any pressing personal problems but because he thought it would help him professionally. In this particular session, he begins with a fantasy he had while he was in a bus. The fantasy was of a tribe living in the jungle which unclothes its dead and hangs them on the trees. Mohan, the patient, visualized a beautiful woman hanging on one of the trees. He imagined himself coming at night and having intercourse with the woman. Other members of the tribe are eating parts of the hanging corpses. The fantasy is immediately followed by the recollection of an incident from the previous evening. Mohan was visiting his parents' home where he had lived till recently when he married and set up his own household. This step was not only personally painful but also unusual for his social milieu where sons normally brought their wives to live in their parental home. His younger sister, with her three-year-old son, was also visiting at the same time. Mohan felt irritated by the anxious attention his mother and grandmother gave the boy. The grandmother kept telling the child not to go and play outside the house, to be careful of venturing too far and so on. On my remarking that perhaps he recognized himself in the nephew, Mohan exclaimed with rare resentment, 'Yes, all the women [his mother, grandmother, his father's brother's wife and his father's unmarried sister who lived with them] were always doing the same with me'.

Beginning with these ten minutes of a session, I would like to unroll Mohan's conflicts around maternal representations and weave them together with the central maternal configurations of Indian culture. Because of his particular objective, my presentation of further material from Mohan's analysis is bound to be subject to what Donald Spence (1986) has called 'narrative smoothing'. A case history, though it purports to be a story that is true, is actually always at the intersection of fact and fable. Its tale quality, though, arises less from the commissions in imagination than from omissions in reality.

Born in a lower-middle-class family in a large village near Delhi, Mohan is the eldest of three brothers and two sisters. His memories of growing up, till well into youth, are pervaded by the maternal phalanx of the four women. Like his mother, who in his earliest memories stands out as a distinct figure from a maternal–feminine continuum to be then reabsorbed into it, Mohan, too, often emerges from and retreats into femininity. In the transference, the fantasies of being a woman are not especially disturbing; neither are the fantasies of being an infant suckling at a breast which he has grown on to my exaggeratedly hairy chest. One of his earliest recollections is of a woman who used to pull at the penises of the little boys playing out in the street. Mohan never felt afraid when the woman grabbed at his own penis. In fact, he rather liked it, reassured that he had a penis at all or at least enough of one for the woman to acknowledge its existence.

Bathed, dressed, combed and caressed by one or the other of the women, Mohan's wishes and needs were met before they were even articulated. Food, especially the milk-based Indian sweets, was constantly pressed on him. Even now, on his visits to the family, the first question by one of the women pertains to what he would like to eat. For a long time during the analysis, whenever a particular session was stressful because of what he considered a lack of maternal empathy in my interventions, Mohan felt compelled to go to a restaurant in town where he would first gorge himself on sweets before he returned home.

Besides the omnipresence of women, my most striking impressions of Mohan's early memories is their diurnal location in night and their primarily tactile quality. Partly, this has to do with the crowded, public living arrangements of the Indian family. Here, even the notions of privacy are absent, not to speak of such luxuries as separate bedrooms for parents and children. Sleeping in the heat with little or no clothes next to one of his caretakers, an arm or a leg thrown across the maternal body, there is one disturbing memory which stands out clearly. This is of Mohan's penis erect against the buttocks of his sleeping mother and his reluctance to move away struggling against the feelings of shame and embarrassment that she may wake up and notice the forbidden touch. Later, in adolescence, the mothers are replaced by visiting cousins sharing mattresses spread out in the room or on the roof, furtive rubbings of bodies and occasional genital contact while other members of the extended family were in various stages of sleep.

Embedded in this blissful abundance of maternal flesh and promiscuity of touch, however, is a nightmare. Ever since childhood and persisting well into the initial phases of the analysis, Mohan would often scream in his sleep while a vague, dark shape threatened to envelop him. At these times only his father's awakening him with the reassurance that everything was all right helped Mohan compose himself for renewed slumber. The father, a gentle, retiring man who left early in the morning for work and returned home late at night, was otherwise a dim figure hovering at the outskirts of an animated family life.

In the very first sessions of the analysis, Mohan talked of a sexual compulsion which he found embarrassing to acknowledge. The compulsion consisted of travelling in a crowded bus and seeking to press close to the hips of any plump, middle-aged woman standing in the aisle. It was vital for his ensuing excitement that the woman have her back to him. If she ever turned to face Mohan, with the knowledge of his desire in her eyes, his erection immediately subsided and he would hurriedly move away with intense feelings of shame. After marriage, too, the edge of his desire was often at its sharpest when his wife slept on her side with her back to him. In mounting excitement, Mohan would rub against her and want to make love when she was still not quite awake. If, however, the wife gave intimation of becoming an enthusiastic partner in the exercise, Mohan sometimes ejaculated prematurely or found his erection precipitately shrivel.

It is evident from these brief fragments of Mohan's case history that his desire is closely connected with some of the most inert parts of a woman's body, hips and buttocks. In other words, the desire needs the woman to be sexually dead for its fulfilment. The genesis of the fantasy of the hanging corpse with whom Mohan has intercourse at night has at its root the fear of the mothers' sexuality as well as the anger at their restraint on his explorations of the world. My choice of Mohan's case, though, is not dictated by the interest it may hold from a psychoanalytical perspective. The choice, instead, has to do with its central theme, namely the various paths in imagination which Mohan traverses, in face of many obstacles, to maintain an idealized relationship with the maternal body. This theme and the fantasized solutions to the disorders in the mother–son relationship are repeated again and again in Indian case and life histories. Bose's observation on the Indian male patient's 'primitive idea of being a woman' is then only a special proposition of a more general theorem. The wish to be a woman is one particular solution to the discord that threatens the breaking up of the son's fantasized connection to the mother, a solution whose access to awareness is facilitated by the culture's views on sexual differentiation and the permeability of gender boundaries. Thus, for instance, when Gandhi (1943) publicly proclaims that he has mentally become a woman or, quite unaware of Karen Horney and other deviants from the orthodox analytic position of the time, talks of man's envy of the woman's procreative capacities, saying 'There is as much reason for a man to wish that he was born a woman as for woman to do otherwise', he is sure of a sympathetic and receptive audience.

In the Indian context, this particular theme can be explored in individual stories as well as in the cultural narratives as we call myths, both of which are more closely interwoven in Indian culture than is the case in the modern West. In an apparent reversal of a Western pattern, traditional myths in India are less a source of intellectual and aesthetic satisfaction for the mythologist than of emotional recognition for others, more moving for the patient than for the analyst. Myths in India are not part of a bygone era. They are not '*retained* fragments from the infantile psychic life of the race' as Karl Abraham (1913, p. 72) called them or '*vestiges* of the infantile fantasies of whole nations, secular dreams of youthful humanity' in Freud's words (Freud, 1908, p. 152). Vibrantly alive, their symbolic power intact, Indian myths constitute a cultural idiom which aids the individual in the construction and integration of his inner world. Parallel to pattern of infant care and to the structure and values of family relationships, popular and well-known myths are iso-morphic with the central psychological constellations of the culture and are constantly renewed and validated by the nature of subjective experi-ence (Obeyesekere, 1981). Given the availability of the mythological idiom, it is almost as easy to mythologize a psychoanalysis, such as that of Mohan, as to analyse a myth; almost as convenient to elaborate on intrapsychic conflict in a mythological mode as it is in a case–historical narrative mode.

Earlier, I advanced the thesis that the myths of Devi, the great goddess, constitute a 'hegemonic narrative' of Hindu culture. Of the hundreds of myths on her various manifestations, my special interest here is in the goddess as mother, and especially the mother of the sons, Ganesha and Skanda. But before proceeding to connect Mohan's tale to the larger cultural story, let me note that I have ignored the various versions of these myths in traditional texts and modern folklore—an undertaking which is rightly the preserve of mythologists and folklorists—and instead picked on their best-known, popular versions.

The popularity of Ganesha and Skanda as gods—psychologically re-presenting two childhood positions of the Indian son—is certainly undeniable. Ganesha, the remover of obstacles and the god of all begin-nings, is perhaps the most adored of the reputed 330 million Hindu gods. Iconically represented as a pot-bellied toddler with an elephant head and one missing tusk, he is represented proportionately as a small child when portrayed in the family group with his mother Parvati and father Shiva. His image, whether carved in stone or drawn up in a coloured print, is everywhere: in temples, homes, shops, roadside shrines, calendars. Ganesha's younger brother Skanda or Kartikkeya, has his own following, especially in South India where he is extremely popular and worshipped under the name of Murugan or Subramanya. In contrast to Ganesh, Skanda is a handsome child, a youth of slender body and heroic exploits who in analytic parlance may be said to occupy the phallic position.

Ganesha's myths tell us one part of Mohan's inner life while those of Skanda reveal yet another. Ganesha, in many myths, is solely his mother Parvati's creation. Desirous of child and lacking Shiva's cooperation in the venture, she created him out of the dirt and sweat of her body mixed with unguents. Like Mohan's fantasies of his femininity, Ganesha too is not only his mother's boy but contains her very essence. Mohan, even while indubitably male like Skanda, is immersed in the world of mothers which an Indian extended family creates for the child. Skanda, like Mohan, is the son of more than one mother: his father Shiva's seed being too powerful could not be borne by one woman and wandered from womb to womb before Skanda took birth. Mohan's ravenous consumption of sweets to restore feelings of well-being has parallels with Ganesha's appetite for *modakas*, the sweet wheat or rice balls which devotees offer to the god in large quantities, 'knowing' that the god is never satisfied, that his belly empties itself as fast as it is filled (Courtright, 1986, p. 114). For, like the lean Mohan, the fat god's sweets are a lifeline to the mother's breast; his hunger for the mother's body, in spite of temporary appeasements, is ultimately doomed to remain unfulfilled. Mohan is further like Ganesha in that he too has emerged from infancy with an ample capacity for vital involvement with others.

In the dramatization of Mohan's dilemma in relation to the mother, brought to a head by developmental changes that push the child towards an exploration of the outer world while they also give him increasing intimations of his biological rock-bottom identity as a male, Ganesha and Skanda play the leading roles. In a version common to both South India and Sri Lanka (Obeyesekere, 1984) the myth is as follows:

A mango was floating down the stream and Uma (Parvati), the mother, said that whoever rides around the universe first will get the mango [in other versions, the promise is of *modakas* or wives]. Skanda impulsively got on his golden peacock and went around the universe. But Ganesha, who rode the rat, had more wisdom. He thought: 'What could my mother have meant by this?' He then circumambulated his mother, worshipped her and said, 'I have gone around my universe.' Since Ganesha was right his mother gave him the mango. Skanda was furious when he arrived and demanded the mango. But before he could get it Ganesha bit the mango and broke one of his tusks (p. 471).

Here Skanda and Ganesha are personifications of the two opposing wishes of the older child on the eve of the Oedipus complex. He is torn between a powerful push for independent and autonomous functioning and an equally strong pull toward surrender and re-immersion in the enveloping maternal fusion from which he has just emerged. Giving in to the pull of individuation and independence, Skanda becomes liable to one kind of punishment—exile from the mother's bountiful presence, and one kind of reward—the promise of functioning as an adult, virile man. Going back to the mother—and I would view Ganesha's eating of the mango as a return to and feeding at the breast, especially since we know that in Tamil Nadu the analogy between a mango and the breast is a matter of common awareness (Egnor, 1984, p. 15)—has the broken tusk, the loss of potential masculinity, as a consequence. Remaining an infant, Ganesha's reward, on the other hand, will be never to know the pangs of separation from the mother, never to feel the despair at her absence. That Ganesha's lot is considered superior to Skanda's is perhaps an indication of the Indian man's cultural preference in the dilemma of separation–individuation. He is at one with his mother in her wish not to have the son separate from her, individuate out of their shared anima (Kakar, 1987).

For Mohan, as we have seen, the Ganesha position is often longed for and sometimes returned to in fantasy. It does not, however, represent an enduring solution to the problem of maintaining phallic desire in the face of the overwhelming inner presence of the Great Mother. Enter Skanda. After he killed the demon Taraka who had been terrorizing the gods, the goddess became quite indulgent towards her son and told him to amuse himself as he pleased. Skanda became wayward, his lust rampant. He made love to the wives of the gods and the gods could not stop him. Upon their complaining to the goddess, she decided she would assume the form of whatever woman Skanda was about to seduce. Skanda summoned the wife of one god after another but in each saw his mother and became passionless. Finally thinking that 'the universe is filled with my mother' he decided to remain celibate for ever.

Mohan, too, we saw, became 'passionless' whenever the motherly woman he fancied in the bus turned to face him. But, instead of celibacy, he tried to hold on to desire by killing the sexual part of the mother, deadening the lower portion of her trunk, which threatened him with impotence. Furthermore, the imagined sexual overpoweringness of the mother, in the face of which the child feels hopelessly inadequate, with fears of being engulfed and swallowed by her dark depth, is not experienced by Mohan in the form of clear-cut fantasies but in a recurrent nightmare from which he wakes up screaming. Elsewhere, I have traced in detail the passage of the powerful, sexual mother through Hindu myths, folk beliefs, proverbs, symptoms and the ritual worship of the goddess in her terrible and fierce forms (Kakar, 1978). Here, I shall only narrate one of the better-known myths of Devi, widely reproduced in her iconic representations in sculpture and painting, in order to convey through the myth's language of the concrete, of image and symbol, some of the quality of the child's awe and terror of this particular maternal image.

The demon Mahisasura had conquered all the three worlds. Falling in love with the goddess, he sent a message to make his desire known to her. Devi replied that she would accept as her husband only someone who defeated her in battle. Mahisasura entered the battlefield with a vast army and a huge quantity of fighting equipment. Devi came alone, mounted on her lion. The gods were surprised to see her without even an armour, riding naked to the combat. Dismounting, Devi started dancing and cutting off the heads of millions and millions of demons with her sword to the rhythm of her movement. Mahisasura, facing death, tried to run away by becoming an elephant. Devi cut off his trunk. The elephant became a buffalo and against its thick hide Devi's sword and spear were of no avail. Angered, Devi jumped on the buffalo's back and rode it to exhaustion. When the buffalo demon's power of resistance had collapsed, Devi plunged her spear into its ear and Mahisasura fell dead.

The myth is stark enough in its immediacy and needs no further gloss on the omnipotence and sexual energy of the goddess, expressed in the imagery of her dancing and riding naked, exhausting even the most powerful male to abject submission and ultimately death, decapitating (i.e. castrating) millions of 'bad boys' with demonic desires, and so on. The only feature of the myth I would like to highlight, and which is absent both in Mohan's case vignette and in the myths narrated so far is that of the sword- and spear-wielding Devi as the phallic mother. In the Indian context, this fantasy seems more related to Chasseguet-Smirgel's (1964) notion of the phallic mother being a denial of the adult vagina and the feelings of inadequacy it invokes rather than allowing its traditional interpretation as a denial of castration anxiety. In addition I would see the image of the goddess as man–woman (or, for the matter, of Shiva as *ardhanarishwara*, half man–half woman) as incorporating the boy's wish to become a man without having to separate and sexually differentiate from the mother, to take on male sexual attributes while not letting go the female ones.

The myth continues that when Devi's frenzied dancing did not come to an end even after the killing of the buffalo demon, the gods became alarmed and asked Shiva for help. Siva lay down on his back and when the goddess stepped on her husband she hung out her tongue in shame and stopped. Like Mohan's gentle and somewhat withdrawn father who was the only one who could help in dissipating the impact of the nightmare, Shiva too enters the scene supine yet a container for the great mother's energy and power. In other words, the father may be unassuming and remote, yet powerful. First experienced as an ally and a protector (or even as a co-victim), the father emerges as a rival only later. The rivalry too, in popular Indian myths and most of the case histories, is not so much that of Oedipus, where the power of the myth derives from the son's guilt over a fantasized and eventually unconscious parricide. The Indian context stresses more the father's envy of what belongs to the son—including the mother—and thus the son's persecution anxiety as a primary motivation in the father–son relationship. It is thus charged with the fear of filicide and with the son's castration, by self or the father, as solution to father-son competition, Shiva's beheading of Ganesha who on the express wish of his mother stood guard at her private chambers while she bathed, and the replacement of his head by that of an elephant, the legends of Bhishma and Puru, who renounced sexual functioning in order to keep the affections of their fathers intact, are some of the better-known illustrations (Kakar and Ross, 1987). But the fate of fathers and sons and families and daughters are different narratives; stories yet to be told, texts still to be written.

The importance of the Oedipus complex in classical psychoanalysis lies not only in it being a dominant organizing pattern of a boy's object relations but also in it being the fulcrum of Freud's cultural theory. Freud considered the myth of Oedipus as a hegemonic narrative of all cultures at all times although enough evidence is now available to suggest that its dominance may be limited to some Western cultures at certain periods of their history. In other words, the Oedipus complex, in one variation or the other, may well be universal but not equally hegemonic across cultures. Similarly, I suggest, the Ganesha complex discussed in this essay together with its myth, is equally universal at a certain stage of the male child's development. It is a mythologem for relations between mother and child at the eve of Oedipus before any significant triangulation has taken place. The Ganesha complex, I have tried to show, is also the hegemonic developmental narrative of the male self in Hindu India. In another of its variations as the Ajase complex, it has also been postulated as the dominant narrative of the male self in Japan.

Culture and Human Development

Cultural ideas and ideals, manifested in their narrative form as myths, are the innermost experience of the self. One cannot therefore speak of an 'earlier' or 'deeper', of the self beyond cultural reach. As a 'depth psychology', psychoanalysis dives deep but in the same waters in which the cultural rivers too flow. Pre-eminently operating from within the heart of the Western Myth, enclosed in the *mahamaya* of Europe—from myths of ancient Greece to the 'illusions' of the Enlightenment—psychoanalysis has had little opportunity to observe from within, and with empathy, the deeper import of other cultures' myths in the workings of the self.

The questions relating to the 'how' of this process are bound up with the larger issue of the relationship between the inner and outer worlds which has been of perennial psychological and philosophical interest. It is certainly not my intention to discuss these questions at any length. I would only like to point out that apart from some notable exceptions, such as Erik Erikson (1950) who both held aloft and significantly contributed to a vision of a 'psychoanalysis sophisticated enough to include the environment', the impact of culture on the development of a sense of identity—in the construction of the self, in modern parlance—has been generally underestimated. Freud's 'timetable' of culture entering the psychic structure relatively late in life as 'ideology' of the superego (Freud, 1922) has continued to be followed by other almanac makers of the psyche. Even Heinz Kohut, as Janis Long (1986) has shown, does not quite follow the logical implications of his concept of 'selfobject'. These are, of course, the aspects of the other which are incorporated in the self and are experienced as part of one's own subjectivity. Kohut, too, follows Freud in talking of a 'culture selfobject' of later life (Kohut, 1985), derived in part from cultural ideas and ideals, which helps in maintaining the integrity and vitality of the individual self. Yet the idea of selfobject which goes beyond the notion of a budding self's relatedness to the environment, to the environment's gradual transmutation into *becoming* the self implies that '*what* the parents respond to in a developing child, *how* they respond and what they present as idealizable from the earliest age' (Long, 1986, p. 8)—surely much of it a cultural matter—will be the raw material for the child's inner construction of the self. In other words, a caretaker's *knowing* of the child, a knowing in which affect and cognition are ideally fused, is in large part cultural and forms the basis of the child's own knowing of his or her self. The notion that the construction and experience of the self is greatly influenced by culture from the very beginning does not imply that there is no difference between individual faces and cultural masks, no boundary between inner and outer worlds. The tension between the two is what gives psychoanalysis and literature much of their narrative power. What I seek to emphasize here is that this boundary cannot be fixed either in time or psychic space. It is dynamic, mobile and constantly subject to change.

Summary

Interweaving myths and case history, this paper argues that given the non-Western nature of the family environment in India, certain aspects of the powerful mother (-goddess) have a great impact on the development of the male child. Defensively the Hindu boy copes with this figure of intense import in certain culturally favoured ways, e.g. by remaining tied to the infantile position, celibacy or impotence as a defence against phallic licence, retaining a degree of potency by deadening the mother, identification with the mother and so on. Moreover, the role of the father too has a specific cultural configuration. The paper further argues that the construction and experience of the self are influenced by culture from the very beginning of life and that analysts have generally placed its influence too late in the developmental timetable.

REFERENCES

Abraham, K. (1913), *Dreams and Myths: A Study in Race Psychology*, New York: Journal of Nervous and Mental Health Publishing Company.
Bose, G. (1948), 'A New Theory of Mental Life', *Samiksa*, 2: 108–205.
——— (1949), 'The Genesis and Adjustment of the Oedipus Wish', *Samiksa*, 3: 222–40.
——— (1950), 'The Genesis of Homosexuality', *Samiksa*, 4: 66–85.
Chasseguet-Smirgel, J. (1964), 'Feminine Guilt and the Oedipus Complex', in J. Chasseguet-Smirgel ed., *Female Sexuality*, Ann Arbor: Univ. Michigan Press.
Courtright, P. (1986), *Ganesa*, New York: Oxford Univ. Press.
Egnor, M. (1984), *The Ideology of Love in a Tamil Family*, unpublished manuscript: Hobart & Smith College.
Erikson, E. (1950), *Childhood and Society*, New York: Norton.

Freud, S. (1908), 'Creative Writers and Daydreaming', *S.E.* 9.

———— (1922), 'New Introductory Lectures on Psychoanalysis, *S.E.* 22.

Kakar (1978), *The Inner World: A Psychoanalytic Study of Childhood and Society in India*, Delhi and New York: Oxford Univ. Press.

———— (1987), 'Psychoanalysis and Anthropology: A Renewed Alliance', *Contributions to Indian Sociology*, 21: 85–8.

———— and Ross, J. M. (1987), *Tales of Love, Sex and Danger*, London: Unwin Hyman.

Kohut, H. (1985), *Self Psychology and the Humanities*, New York: Norton.

Long, J. (1986), 'Culture, Selfobject and the Cohesive Self', unpublished paper presented at American Psychological Association Meeting.

Obeyesekere, G. (1981), *Medusa's Hair*, Chicago: Univ. of Chicago Press.

———— (1984), *The Cult of Pattini*, Chicago: Univ. of Chicago Press.

Sinha, T. C. (1966), 'Psychoanalysis in India', in *Lumbini Park Silver Jubilee Souvenir*. Calcutta: Lumbini Park.

Spence, D. P. (1986), 'Narrative Smoothing and Clinical Wisdom', in T. Sarbin ed., *Narrative Psychology*, New York: Praeger.

7

Maternal Enthrallment:
Two Case Histories

These are the first published cases of what I later suggested is perhaps the major male complex in Indian (Hindu) culture and which I have called 'maternal enthrallment'. I have included these cases here (which I would write from a more interactionist perspective today) not because they add conceptually to the discussion in the earlier chapters but because they give narrative life to the paradoxical abstractions of maternal enthrallment: the wish to get away from the mother together with the dread of separation, hate for the mother one longs for so much, incestuous desire (and near-incestuous experiences) coexisting with the terror inspired by assertive female sexuality.

Deven*

In March 1976, the twenty-six year old Deven was referred to me by the trainer of a sensitivity group which Deven had attended a few months back. In the first interview Deven's hair was uncombed, he was shabbily dressed and generally gave the appearance of personal neglect. He spoke haltingly and wept often as he narrated how he had been very dejected since the last three months after he had broken off his engagement. He complained of feelings of deep inferiority, inadequacy and general worthlessness. He thought constantly of suicide, had completely lost interest in his work as a systems engineer, and felt apathetic towards the very real possibility that he might lose his job.

During the interview, he complained of a harsh and authoritarian father who 'has completely ruined my life'. His tone of voice was weepy and whining and near the end of the interview he spoke of a servant who had forced him into a homosexual relationship when he was five years old: 'Both (the father and the servant) have completely ruined my life and

*Revised version of a paper first published as 'A Case of Depression', *Samiksa*, 33(3), 1979, 61–71.

I do not know if I should keep on living.' In spite of the strong depressive affect, Deven was articulate and willing to see his problems in the context of his life history. My initial opinion was that he was suitable for psycho-analysis: his central symptoms of general loss of interest, mental and physical inability to relate to people and enjoy life, corresponded to the impoverishment of the ego in neurotic depression.

A Brahmin by caste, Deven hails from a village in Bihar. His fifty-year-old father is a police inspector in charge of the village *thana*. Both his grandfathers had been poor farmers. Deven is the eldest son and spent the first three years of his life with his mother at the home of his maternal grandfather. His memories of this period are hazy but wrapped in the golden glow of a 'lost paradise'. He remembers being made much of by his mother and his grandparents since he was the only child in this house-hold. His father, who was at that time a police constable in a different village, visited the family only occasionally.

When he was three years old, Deven and his mother moved to the father's house. His memories of this period—from three to five years—as they gradually emerged in the analysis, are quite sharp. Deven was very unhappy at having to share his mother with his stranger father. He re-members constant fights between his parents. In these fights the father, who always had a very short temper, got enraged and beat the mother. Deven also remembers often being beaten by his father. After these fights, the mother would take the son to her breast and would cry, telling him that she was only waiting for him to grow up and become a 'big man' when she would leave the father and move away with her son. It was also during this period—from three to five years—that his younger sister and younger brother were born. Two other siblings, a nine year younger brother and a ten year younger sister followed. Ever since the age of five, Deven fantasized about taking his mother away to live with him. Very recently, about six months before the analysis started, he was able to fulfill this childhood fantasy briefly when he started working in Delhi and asked his mother and younger sister to come and stay with him for a while. However, for the one month that his mother stayed with him he felt irritated and depressed, feeling relieved when she went back to his father. He felt that during this month the mother compared him des-paragingly to his father and often communicated to Deven, sometimes in these very words, that the father was the 'better man'.

At the age of five years, when his parents were away from home, Deven was forced by a servant in whose charge he had been left, to masturbate and suck the man's penis. Deven had been very attached to this servant who had given him much affection during this difficult period of his life. The servant threatened Deven with dire consequences if he dared to report the incident to his father. Deven kept quiet and for the next five to six years, till he was ten years old, the homosexual relationship with the servant continued.

Deven did very well at school, always standing first in his class. Although the fights between his parents continued and he was occasionally beaten by his father, his relationship with his father became better. The father appreciated his son's achievements at school while the son also started admiring the father who had been promoted to sub-inspector and was thus looked upon as a minor god by the villagers. Yet in spite of always standing first in his class, Deven had constant feelings of being inferior and inadequate. Ever since the age of five, he felt that his penis was too small and 'bent'. The worry about his penis soon spread to his whole body. In contrast to his strong, policeman father, Deven felt he was weak and lacked strength. He was very ashamed of his squint, about which he was teased at school, though later the squint was corrected by an eye operation.

At the age of eleven, Deven left home to live with his uncle's family in a small town. The move was dictated by the lack of educational opportunity in the village. Deven remembers this period, till the end of his schooling, as being one of the unhappiest times of his life. His uncle's two sons, sixteen and fourteen years-old, bullied him and often beat him. They also forced him into a passive homosexual role, with anal intercourse, and then spread the word in school that he was a *gandu*, a passive homosexual. Thus in school there were many sexual advances made to him by the older boys who threatened him with physical assault if he did not submit to their demands. Deven resisted these demands but lived with a constant fear of being assaulted and with an overwhelming sense of shame at being branded a *gandu*. The only bright spot in this period were his studies in which, supported and encouraged by one of his teachers, he did extremely well. The teacher often took him for long walks, talking of history and Hindi literature, and painted bright pictures of a successful future for the young boy. After two miserable years with his uncle's family, he insisted to his father that he would like to live alone. The latter arranged for him to have a room in the town's police mess. Deven, free of the unwelcome company of his cousins, lived a lonely life for the next three years, concentrating on his studies, visiting his teacher and longing for the school vacations when he could go home to his family.

Having done very well at the school-leaving examinations, Deven was admitted to the Mechanical Engineering course of the Indian Institute of Technology (IIT) in Bombay. At IIT, he was very shy, feeling like a rustic in the middle of sophisticated city people, and generally kept to himself. If people looked at him for a longer time than was merited by a casual glance, he had the feeling that they were commenting adversely on him. He made very few friends and generally remained in the background, working hard at his studies. He again did well at all his examinations and this intellectual success brought him the esteem of his fellow students who began to seek him out for help in academic tasks.

In his fourth year at IIT, however, Deven had what he calls his first 'breakdown'. The 'breakdown' occurred just six weeks before his final examination and for a while he was certain that he would not be in a position to appear for the examination. The symptoms of the breakdown were a sudden loss of interest in his studies and a general feeling of apathy. He could not sleep at night and would sit for hours, an open book in front of him, mechanically turning over the pages. Although he had regularly been masturbating since his fifteenth year—with feelings of shame, depletion and emptiness after the act—his masturbation became almost compulsive during the depressive episode, which lasted right up to the examinations. During the analysis Deven recalled that in the period preceding the depression he had been assigned a new roommate. This boy was smart, handsome and very sophisticated, and with seemingly little effort he did consistently well in his studies; in fact, he did even better than Deven. He was also the president of the students union, a very good sportsman and the centre of a circle of admiring students. Deven remembers his roommate being consistently nice to him and paying him flattering attention. Yet he also remembers that he was envious of his roommate's easy success and especially of his strong, handsome body which he got to know well in the casual intimacy of a shared room. Deven was able to sit for his examinations, although he did not fare as well as was his wont. During the vacations he slowly recovered and was able to resume his studies for the final year.

After finishing his studies, Deven got a good job in Delhi as a systems analyst. He set up a house of his own and, after living alone for a few months, invited his mother and youngest sister to come and live with him, ostensibly so that his sister, who was thirteen years old, could go to a good school. Although he had at last fulfilled his fantasy of rescuing his mother from his 'harsh authoritarian' father, he found himself feeling irritable and then more and more depressed. In the meantime, his father had fixed up his marriage and Deven had not been able to question or refuse his father's decision. His mother went back soon to make the wedding arrangements. As the day of the marriage approached, Deven found himself getting more and more anxious, convinced that he was impotent with a girl and suffered from premature ejaculation. His panic increased till one day he telegraphed his father that the engagement should be broken off. His father came to Delhi to talk to him but seeing Deven's state, he seemed to have been quite understanding and accepted his son's decision without trying to put too much pressure on him. Deven now felt more and more depressed, worthless and inadequate and unable to work at his job. Sleeplessness and fits of crying increased and he often contemplated suicide. Warned by his boss that his work and its quality had deteriorated greatly, he finally wrote to the trainer of the sensitivity training group he had attended while studying at Bombay, and was referred to me for treatment.

In the first phase of the analysis, Deven spoke haltingly, with long silences and bouts of weeping as he recalled childhood incidents with his father. In all these incidents, the father was portrayed as a tyrant with Deven and his mother as the tyrant's victims. He wept often but the weeping was an angry one, full of self-loathing. He compared himself to a frightened mouse in the presence of his father and felt that this trait had persisted all through his life. If anyone argues loudly, he said, especially, my boss, I have to agree with the person and cannot say what I believe to be true. In these sessions it became clear that Deven's fear of his father had largely to do with his sexual impulses. Whenever he talked of his attraction towards some girl or of his masturbation, it was in a very low, 'mouse-like' voice which I could hardly hear and this happened almost always at the end of the session when he could get away quickly. After any such confession, he would close his eyes tightly, clasp his hands on his stomach in an attitude of praying and cross his legs, as if protecting his genitals from retaliation.

His first reported dream, in the fifteenth session, is as follows:

I was in an unknown city, waiting on a street for transport. A double-decker bus comes but the conductor closes its doors before I can enter and the bus drives away. However, a white Fiat car stops and it is being driven by my managing director. I take the driver's seat and give the MD a lift.

His associations to the dream, though meagre are significant: the 'unknown' city is Calcutta which Deven had recently visited and where he had 'lost his pen'; the bus-conductor was wearing a khaki uniform 'like a policeman'. The white Fiat car is, of course, mine which he passes on the driveway when he comes for analysis. In my interpretation, I emphasize the positive transference by relating the dream to his wish and hope to find his way through his unknown 'inner city' in my car but with him in the 'driver's seat'.

The theme of the analysis, roughly till the eightieth session, centres around the problem of his ambivalent feelings toward his father. With the strengthening of the therapeutic alliance he lets himself experience the extent of his rage towards his father as he remembers his feelings of helplessness when his father hit his mother or thrashed him. Most of the memories of his father's 'tyranny' are early ones, when he was between three to seven years old, and he begins to realize their origin in the rage at the father for breaking the 'blissful' mother–son dyad when mother and son went to live with the father for the first time when Deven was three years old. He dreams of an office party in which his boss takes away the prettiest women for a dance while Deven looks on and then everyone screams as an earthquake shakes the dance floor. Whereas up to now, I had been the loving, soothing, giving mother in the transference, with an increasing relaxation of the superego he permits himself expressions of rage: once, when I am late for a session, he fantasizes blowing up my car and raping my wife.

As the analysis progresses, Deven discovers that under the overt hostility against the father, there are also considerable feelings of tenderness, affection and admiration. There are memories of walks with the father when Deven was a boy, of Deven visiting the police station and admiring the authoritative efficiency with which the father disposed of his work. There are memories of the father's booming laughter, his zest for life and his constant encouragement and appreciation of the son's academic achievements at school and college. Concomitantly, the mother's image is changing to a devouring and castrating woman who clung to her son, used Deven for her own purposes in the battle against the father and often mocked her son's efforts at individuation. Deven remembers some incidents during childhood which make it clear that many of the beatings he received from his father were at the instigation of his mother. Other childhood recollections make it doubtful whether the mother really hated his father (and only loved her son) as she had claimed and he had believed for such a long time. It seems that many of the cries which he had heard while she was closeted alone with the father, were those of sexual pleasure rather than screams of pain at being beaten. He discovers the extent of his disappointment with the mother especially after the birth of his siblings—another proof of his mother's 'infidelity' with the father.

The great disappointment in the mother during the Oedipal period had led Deven to change his love object. With his strong pre-Oedipal identification with the mother, he turned to his father in a passive, homosexual way, wanting to be sexually loved by his father as he (the father) did Deven's mother. Here is a typical dream fragment during this period of analysis:

I am driving a motor cycle through a crowded place. My father is riding the pillion seat which seems to be suspended a little above its normal position. We are driving fast and it's an exhilarating feeling.

In his associations to this dream, Deven tells of his feelings of discomfort whenever he slept with his father. He used to feel particularly uncomfortable when he had his back to his father and often slept at the edge of the bed. The homosexual wishes toward the father and the attendant anxiety are increasingly expressed toward me in the transference. He talks of the tightening of his anal sphincter when he is lying on the couch and his fantasy that I might get up from my chair to assault him. The sexual assault by the servant when he was five years old and the consequent homosexual relationship till he was ten is now often at the forefront of consciousness and is not accompanied by strong anxiety reactions characteristic of the early days of analysis. Deven sees that his passive homosexual wishes were displaced from the father to the servant, a situation in which the adult exploited the child for the satisfaction of his own libidinous needs. In the transference, I often become the servant as Deven lies rigidly, seemingly poised to leap up from the couch and take flight at the slightest threat from my direction. He dreams:

You (the analyst) are sitting against a wall. There is a yellow cloth covering your legs. You have an expression on your face as if saying 'I have got you'.

Association reveal that the fantasied facial expression on my face is that of the servant when he used to take off his underpants and the yellow cloth is the one with which the servant used to wipe off the semen after

Deven had masturbated him. Deven remembers hating the touch and the smell of that cloth, a smell which suddenly becomes very vivid. Deven can now relate his passive-homosexual impulses to his first depressive episode at the Indian Institute of Technology (IIT), where these strivings were activated in relation to the roommate and were accompanied by the feelings of his not being a man. Deven's feelings of being worthless (and its underlying unconscious fantasy of being castrated), alternating with pride in his intellectual capabilities and academic achievements, is another major theme throughout the analysis. The feelings of worthlessness are related to a defective body image, to Deven's conviction during childhood that his penis is 'bent' and that he a 'weakling' as compared to his sturdy policeman father. This feeling of insufficiency is ultimately related to the mother's lack of acceptance and understanding of the child as he was, and her constant exhortations that Deven should become adult soon, become 'bigger than the father' and take her away to live with him. In fact, just before his depressive episode, when his mother left him to go back to his father she had said, 'You may be very educated and everything else but your father is any day a bigger man than you will ever be.'

In the outer world, Deven is doing very well indeed. After having been given two out-of-turn promotions, he is now in charge of his own group and carries out complicated engineering projects with independent responsibility. He can increasingly think of the prospect of marriage with a degree of equanimity. After examining the various proposals sent to him by his family he finally decides, not without fears of a repetition of his previous depression and the fear of impotence, to get married. In an euphoric state, he reports of a 'problem-less' sexual functioning with his wife and expresses his relief that he is both potent and can be emotionally involved and love a woman. After six weeks of marriage, Deven's wife, according to the customs of his community, has to go and stay with his parents for some time at their village home. The wife's departure triggers off his basic conflict once again though with a tolerable affect level, a considerable degree of insight and an opportunity for a further working through the conflict. He once again has hostile feelings towards the father and fantasizes that the father may rape his wife. Yet these feelings change soon and his ambivalence towards the mother-wife comes out in complaints of missing her sorely yet feeling that the separation is good for him since his wife is sexually insatiable and he has started feeling tired every morning on leaving for work after having been 'forced' to have intercourse during the night. The imagery of the sexually devouring, overpowering mother in whose presence not only the son but also the father is helpless, a mother who mocks her son's pretensions, comes through clearly in a highly significant dream:

I am in our village home when a gang of dacoits led by a girl attack our house. The female leader of the band is chasing me through the rooms of the house. I pass my father in the hall. He is lying on the bed with a gun but his gun is ineffective. I am very afraid as the girl bandit runs after me, laughing and mocking me for not being able to defend myself.

Now in a position to make most of the connections himself, Deven realizes that the imagery of his mother—an ambivalently loved object who was both giving and devouring, who alternately condemned and idealized the child—has started intruding in his relationship with his wife and that the protectors—the father, the analyst—can only be of limited assistance.

Karan*

In this short case history I would like to share some observations on the analysis of a patient with a narcissistic personality disorder which bring a phenomenon I have elsewhere called the 'Oedipal alliance' into sharp focus (Kakar, 1982). 'Oedipal alliance' refers to the deeply buried and unfulfilled need of many male patients for the firm support, guidance and emotional availability of the father who was needed by the little boy at the Oedipal stage of his life, so that the boy could separate and free himself from an overwhelming, omnipresent, and especially the sexually threatening pre-Oedipal mother.

Karan was a forty-year old lecturer at the university who came to analysis with severe anxiety states and obsessive ideas that frightened him even further. In the bathroom, while urinating, the idea would come to him that he should slice off his penis, while a lighted cigarette would bring the idea that he might stub it out in his eyes, thus blinding himself. Karan was frightened that these ideas could develop into uncontrollable urges and of his feeling that he was becoming schizophrenic.

In the first interview, Karan was obviously agitated as he recounted the

*Slightly edited version of a paper first published as 'Observations on the "Oedipal alliance" in a patient with a narcissistic personality disorder', *Samiksa*, 34(2), 1980.

origin of his symptoms. For the last one year, Karan had found himself increasingly involved with a female colleague at the university. The woman, Karan reported, had sought him out and taken the initiative in their relationship which she wanted to turn into a sexual one. Karan was both fascinated and withdrawn; ideas of leaving his wife and four children alternating with intense feelings of guilt and anxiety. His agitation gradually mounted, the obsessive idea around self-castration made their appearance, and when Karan came to see me he was on a fairly high dosage of an anti-psychotic drug that he had been administering to himself for the last fourteen years. The drug had been prescribed by a psychiatrist who had treated Karan for a psychotic episode that had lasted for three days.

As Karan recalled this episode, which was diagnosed as schizophrenia at the time, it had started with intense agitation and a loss of his sense of identity. He had felt that his face had changed into that of a well-known British professor of philosophy who was visiting Delhi. Karan had the feeling that he himself was the author of the books that were displayed in the university lecture hall where the British professor was invited to speak to the faculty. Karan had rushed off to a friend, greatly agitated and in panic. The friend had called his father who tried to calm him down by giving him a glass of water. Karan had the delusion that the father was giving him a glass of whisky to poison him and when he put a calming hand on Karan's shoulder, he reacted violently, thinking that the father wanted to strangle him. Karan was taken to a psychiatrist, given a couple of electric shocks and then put on the anti-psychotic drug. Ever since this episode (which did not recur) Karan was afraid of a psychotic breakdown and for the next fourteen years, daily took a mild dosage of the drug prescribed at that time, increasing the dose whenever he felt his anxiety increase.

For the first few sessions, Karan started each session with a minute discussion of his symptoms, as if lecturing to a group of residents at a psychiatric clinic of which he was the chief. Over the last fourteen years, Karan had read an enormous number of books on psychiatry, psychoanalysis and psychology in an effort to deal with his fear of schizophrenia. It seemed that Karan had experienced his psychotic episode as a narcissistic injury of the first magnitude and had directed much of his effort and considerable intellectual resources in an effort at self-healing. Besides a familiarity with the technical terminology, this unsystematic reading had given Karan a number of different psychiatric explanations for the various mental disorders which he often used indiscriminately in his discourses. Though nominally deferential (he often began a sentence with 'Of course, you know this . . .'), it was evident that Karan considered me a part of a large, appreciative audience to which he expounded the problem of suffering in Existentialism, Buddhism and other philosophical systems of thought. He constantly referred to his writings and books, published, being written or contemplated, while he made use of the first sessions for developing and exhibiting his grandiose self.

Karan was the first-born of a middle-class family in Jaipur that had gone through great financial difficulties when he was in high school, though it had later recovered its fortunes. Karan's portrait of his father was of an imperious patriarch who worked hard, had strict moral standards, but was quite distant from his two sons when they were growing up. Children, the father felt, were a woman's business and he rarely concerned himself with their upbringing. Karan was much more ambivalent about his mother. She seems to have been a beautiful woman, somewhat dreamy and quite self-absorbed. Outwardly a submissive housewife, Karan's mother seemed to have lived in her own fantasy world while the son looked on, fearful and adoring, but always at the edge of her closed world. Overprotective of the child at times and quite indifferent at others, the solipsistic world of Karan's mother baffled the child. It was an uncertain world in which the child could be included and banished at whim. In her old age, Karan's mother was showing distinct signs of odd behaviour, such as hanging her washed underwear out in the open where the neighbours could see it, which acutely embarrassed the family.

In the early stages of the analysis, Karan seemed to relive his relationship with his mother: his discourses were self-absorbed, oblivious of my presence, reflecting his identification with his mother (with me as the child at the edge of her world). Soon, however, Karan's grandiose fantasies about himself began to be mixed with an intense idealization of me. He had read a recent book I had written and to Karan, 'It was the best book he had ever read', 'a work of genius' and so forth. I was the best analyst in the country, a god-like creature possessing attributes of perfection and all extant wisdom. In this primitive self-idealization and idealization of the analyst, Karan recreated those euphoric periods in which as a child he had been included in the mother's narcissistic world which had made him feel 'special' and a part of the mother's 'perfection'. Karan's apparent idealization, however, was interspersed with a hidden devaluation and a subtle derogatory attitude toward me. Thus he would often attack Freud and psychoanalysis from a 'philosophical' and 'moral' viewpoint, taking care to except me from his collective derogation of psychoanalysts. At this stage, I did not interpret either his idealizations or his devaluation, in order to let the idealizing-transference develop more fully. Instead, I concentrated on the interpretation of his obsessive ideas around self-castration.

In adolescence, it seems, from the ages of fourteen to eighteen, Karan had had certain incestuous experiences with his mother. The memories of these experiences were attached to intense feelings of guilt and shame and Karan's agitation was palpable when he recollected these events. Since the family was living in a single room at the time, Karan would lie on the same bed with his mother on many afternoons while his father was away working. While his mother pretended to be asleep, Karan would fearfully rub his erect penis against his mother's thighs and would ejaculate in his trousers. In the analysis, memories came up which made it evident that Karan's mother was not a passive recipient of the boy's sexual attention—as Karan had wanted (and needed) to believe—but in fact actively encouraged her son. She would ask Karan to lock the door against the father's unexpected arrival and often lie on the bed in a way that pulled her *saree* above her thighs. In one of the sessions, which produced great anxiety, Karan recalled for the first time that after he had ejaculated, his mother said to him, 'You satisfy yourself, but you should also take care of me'.

The re-emergence of these memories, I have indicated above, was accompanied by intense anxiety and a succession of dreams in which different men—in relation to whom Karan was servile and ingratiating—threatened him with physical torture or death. His ideas of self-castration were meant to appease the castration threat which had again become acute because of the activation of a feared, yet desired mother-image. The image was incorporated now by the female colleague 'who was trying to seduce him'. This interpretation, and the tracing of its further origins to his incestuous wishes and experiences during adolescence, led to a complete disappearance of these particular symptoms. Karan also recalled that his psychotic episode fourteen years ago had been triggered off by his first 'love affair' with a girl student—an affair that was never consummated but was full of guilty fantasies of seduction and being seduced. I do not, however, propose to dwell on the fate of Karan's castration anxiety or on other personality features which emerged during analysis: his proneness to primary-process thinking when feeling anxious, his lack of impulse control which led him to bouts of drinking and gambling, followed by self-condemnation and feelings of utter worthlessness. My chief interest here is the theme of Oedipal alliance in Karan's life history as it unfolded in the transference situation. For, with the activation of memories of his mother's seductiveness, Karan also began to discover his intense rage towards his mother. Here is a typical dream fragment from this period.

I am walking with my publisher (who was considering Karan's recent book for publication) when we come to some railway tracks and I see a woman lying dead across the tracks, her head severed by a passing train.

Karan's idealization of me now became more marked, his efforts at identification more insistent. Very deferentially, he would seek to elicit my opinions on a variety of moral issues, on the meaning of life and death and other such weighty matters. Lying on the couch, he would often turn his face to look at me, as if reassuring himself on my continued presence and accessibility. This was indeed a change from his earlier self-absorbed soliloquies and his efforts at maintaining intact the grandiose self-image of omniscience and fame. Karan, it seemed to me, was seeking to identify with me as the father who would not only help the boy to deal with his incestuous fantasies but also with his feelings of rage against the threatening mother. Besides trying to deal with the vicissitudes of the Oedipal complex, Karan was also embarked on a desperate search for the Oedipal alliance. The latter is epitomized by one particular session which Karan began with a verbal parapraxis, 'I had an erotic mother'—instead of 'I had an erotic dream'. Karan then went on to describe the dream:

I am lying on my bed when I see my mother approaching. She is almost naked and has a gloating expression on her face. I am very scared. Then I see you (the analyst) sitting in one corner of the room with an enormous erect penis next to your chair that rises from the floor and reaches the ceiling. I hold the penis and feel safe.

Although Karan's sparse associations to the dream brought up the memory of his mother's beautiful breasts and thus hinted at Karan's own feeling of a helpless fear in face of a mother who threatened to engulf his budding individuality, destroy his masculinity, and reflected his need for the father who would help him prevent such a calamity. In my own associations to Karan's dream, I was reminded of a mythological motif, depicted in some old temple relics, in which a boy holds fast to his father's penis to escape Yama, the god of death and the harbinger of that ultimate narcisstic injury—the extinction of the self. In Karan's case, of course, the god of death was a (Mother-) goddess.

In conclusion, let me also note that in Karan's case as in Pran's (Chapter V), manifest sexual stimulation of the boy by the mother is associated more with sexual inhibitions and dysfunctions than with genuine perversions of the kind reported in Western case histories (Bak, 1968; Glasser, 1976; McDougall, 1972).

REFERENCES

Bak, R. C. (1968), 'The Phallic Woman', *The Psychoanalytic Study of the Child,* 23, 15–36.

Glasser, M. (1979), 'Role of Aggression in Perversions', in I. Roven ed., *Sexual Deviations*, Oxford: Oxford Univ. Press.

Kakar, S. (1982), 'Fathers and Sons: The Indian Experience', in S. Cath, A. Gurwit and J. Ross eds, *Father and Child: Developmental and Clinical Perspectives,* Boston: Atlantic Little-Brown.

McDougall, J. (1972), 'Primal Scene and Sexual Perversion', *Int. Journal of Psychoanalysis*, 53, 371–84.

8

The Search for Middle Age
in India

For a while I thought I would never find it. I began looking for middle age in diverse settings by asking people what they thought were the various ages of a person. I remember putting this question to a young boatman in Benares as he took me on a leisurely boat ride down the Ganges, a retired soldier on a bus journey to Bangalore, a well-known (woman) editor of a daily newspaper in Delhi, an unemployed vegetable-seller and his wife and his sister in Hyderabad who I had just finished interviewing on the subject of social violence between Hindus and Muslims. Middle age did not seem to exist or at least it was never spontaneously mentioned as long as my question and the subsequent conversation were in Hindi. I finally discovered its hiding place when at a cocktail party in Delhi, I asked the guests (in English, and sounding faintly Shakespearean) what they thought were the various 'ages of man'. For these upper middle-class men and women, educated in the English-speaking and Westernized milieu of convent and private schools, familiar with popular American and British writings on the stages of life and consuming a steady diet in the English language newspapers and magazines on the middle-age spread and the mid-life crisis, the increased risk of coronary disease in middle age and the problems of menopause, middle age was a familiar concept and a known territory—a Western import that no longer seemed like one.

For their more traditional, Hindi-speaking countrymen and women, an infinitely larger part of the country's population, there were only three ages of a human being: childhood, youth and old age. A wit reduced this

First published in R. Shweder ed., *Mid-life and Other Cultural Fictions*, Chicago: Univ. of Chicago Press (under review). Reprinted with permission.

number further when she remarked: 'All Indians are born old and spend the rest of their lives in getting older.' With my Hindi-speaking respondents, I had to probe further and, in fact, even 'lead the witness' by asking whether there was not a transition period between youth and old age before some of them caught on to my intent and 'remembered' that there was indeed also an *adher-awastha*. The standard dictionary—*Bharat Hindi Kosh*—defined *adher* as 'middle age; declining years', while another dictionary was more concrete in defining it as an adjective for a person between the ages of thirty and fifty. There is also another word for middle age—*prodha*, which the dictionary defines as someone who is 'older, between thirty and fifty; whose intelligence is fully developed; experienced; deep; in the middle years; in the declining years'. In ordinary conversation, though, most would use *prodha* in the sense of a quality of age, namely a wise maturity rather than employing the word to refer to a particular span of years in the second half of life.

The chronological uncertainty in the dictionaries on the years which constitute middle age is matched by the *Dharmashastras*, the semi-sacred books of the Hindus on law and a personal code of conduct which, proceeding from an ideal life span of one hundred years, arrive at a different chronological construction of middle age. In defining the duties and appropriate conduct of the four stages of life—*brahmacharya* (apprentice), *garhasthya* (householder), *vanaprastha* (forest-dweller) and *sanyasa* (renunciant)—middle age can conceivably be considered as equivalent to the *vanaprastha* stage which, the texts assert, lasts from the fiftieth to the seventy-fifth year. Within this wide range which begins at thirty according to modern Hindi lexical usage and ends at seventy-five as envisaged by ancient Sanskrit texts, the idea of middle age seems more and more amorphous, at least as far as chronological age is concerned.

The fluidity of the concept of middle age is further underscored by popular sayings which portray the onset of middle age varying according to gender. *Teesi-kheesi*, for instance is an expression that is used for women. It means that when a woman reaches the age of thirty (*tees*), her face caves in and teeth jut out (*khees*), a sign of old age. A man, on the other hand, is *satha-patha*, signifying that even at sixty (*sath*) he remains a virile youth (*patha*). On the other hand, consistent with the nature of proverbs and popular sayings wherein for almost every pithy assertion there is another one maintaining its opposite, *sathia-jana*, 'to become senile', is a condition which strikes one at sixty.

The question as to what is regarded as middle age in India remains unresolved in social science research as well. Almost all the relevant socio-economic studies (Desai, 1982; de Souza and Fernandes, 1982; Sharma, 1987; Bose and Gangrade, 1988) are concerned with the 'old' or with 'the aging in India'. Given their urban bias, the 'old' are identified as those who have retired from a full-time job, generally government service, where the mandatory retirement age is fifty-eight years. This rough and ready reckoner for the beginning of old age proper and thus, implicitly, the end of middle age, does not apply to women or even 90 per cent of men who do not work in the organized industrial or government sector. The demographers, on the other hand, have age groups based on formal criteria adopted from similar Western studies. This procedure has the virtue of permitting comparisons of the demography of various age groups across the globe but tells us nothing about what Indians consider the middle years of life or whether they consider this period a well defined entity at all.*

Giving up the quest for a precise chronological definition of middle age in India and following the majority of my respondents in viewing it as the beginning of old age, the first act of the drama of the second half of life, the question arises as to what is considered to be the curtain raiser. When and how does middle age come upon us? In Indian terms, what are the heralds of *burhapa*? The answer to this question is clear and consistent through centuries across varied sources which reflect Hindu life and mores—from ancient texts to modern ethnographic accounts. In the religious-ideal image of the *vanaprastha* stage, the curtain rises 'When a householder sees his skin wrinkled, and his hair white, and the sons of his sons, then he may resort to the forest' (Manusmriti, VI.1:2). With characteristic nit-picking, commentators on this pronouncement of Manu, the law-giver, have argued through the centuries whether these are three separate grounds, each sufficient by itself or whether all must exist together. The evidence of modern anthropological studies suggests that today the operative part of Manu's dictum on the beginning of the third quarter of life is not the physical signs of aging but the seeing of 'sons of sons'. In other words, middle age, for both men and women, is marked by their changed roles in the life cycle of the family once the son is

---

*For whatever this information is worth, the middle-aged population of India, according to American demographic criteria, i.e. the 45–59 age group, was 10.33 per cent of the total population in the 1981 census. Currently, this will be about ninety million people.

married, brings his wife home and begins to bear offspring (Fernandez, 1982; Vatuk, 1983). I have a suspicion that it was not much different in ancient times. In the epic of Ramayana, the fateful events of the story are set in motion when King Dashratha sees grey hair on his temples *after* the marriage celebrations of his eldest son, the god-hero of the epic, Rama. In the Hindi version of the epic (Tulsidasa, n.d.), loved and revered throughout the Hindi heartland, 'King Dashratha took a mirror in his hand, saw his face in it and adjusted his crown. He saw that the hair above his ears had become white as if old age is saying, "O King! Make Rama the crown prince and fulfil the purpose of your birth and life" ' (p. 337). The rest—the opposition of Dashratha's youngest wife to this proposal, Rama's fourteen-year exile, the war with the demon king Ravana, and so on—is, as they say, *itihas*—the Hindi word for both history and legend.

Although anthropologists corroborate textual evidence that men and women in India associate the beginning of *burhapa* with the birth of 'sons of sons', I would be inclined to refine this formulation further. From my clinical experience, it is the marriage of the first child—whether son or daughter—and the confrontation with the procreative activity of one's offspring, a sudden not-to-be-repressed awareness of his or her sustained sexual activity, which heralds the psychological transition of men and women into middle age. For the information of incorrigible almanac makers of the life cycle, this event is likely to occur around an average age of forty-five for a man and forty for woman in the urban areas and, reflecting the demographic patterns of marriage in India, a couple of years earlier in the rural population.

Representations of Middle Age in the Hindu Tradition

If, as we saw above, there is a consistency between ancient texts and contemporary accounts of life as lived in the Indian heartland on the markers of middle age, it would be intriguing to discover whether there is a similar continuity in representations of middle age and the main psychological themes of this stage of the life cycle. Let us begin with the 'oughts' of middle age as enumerated by Manu.

Abandoning all food raised by cultivation, and all his belongings, he may depart into the forest, either committing his wife to his sons, or accompanied by her.

Let him offer there five great sacrifices according to the rules, let him wear a skin or tattered garment; let him bathe in the evening or in the morning; the hair on his body, his beard, and his nails unclipped. Let him honor those who come to his hermitage with alms. . . .

Let him always be industrious in privately reciting the Veda; let him be patient of hardship, friendly toward all, of collected mind, giver and never receiver of gifts, and compassionate toward all living creatures (VI.1:3–8).

These verses are followed by others on the importance of restricting diet ('may either eat at night only or in the daytime only') and a list of ascetic practices to be followed, such as exposure to heat in the summer, living under the open sky during the rainy period and dressing in wet clothes during winter. The ascetic regimen and the study of sacred texts prepares a person for the last stage of life and leads to the religiously desired end of a complete union with the supreme Soul (Manusmriti, VI, 1:23:32).

In its religious images, then, middle age constitutes a decisive break in the mode of one's life. It means a withdrawal from family ties and family affairs—the departure for the forest—and a radical renunciation of all worldly concerns and pleasures which were a province of the previous, 'householder' stage. It denotes an end to sexual life since married life is to be continued up to fifty years of age, Manu tells us firmly, and not thereafter. Middle age means an entry into a period of ever increasing asceticism and an involvement with 'ultimate concerns', as the person prepares for the last stage of life and the end of this particular individual life cycle.

We know from other accounts that the religiously desirable radical renunciation was not an unconflicted affair, especially for the rich, the mighty and the powerful, and there were weighty voices in the tradition which opposed this notion of ascetic withdrawal. The fifth-century poet-philosopher Bharatrihari (400 BC?) is a frank sceptic.

Renunciation of worldly attachment
is only talk of scholars,
whose mouths are wordy with wisdom.
Who can really forsake the hips
of beautiful women bound
with girdles of ruby jewels? (p. 82)

I would, therefore, suggest that in the ancient Indian cultural universe there was a specific middle-age crisis of Renunciation vs. Worldly Involvement which is compellingly depicted in an episode from the second great epic of the Hindus, the Mahabharata.

Although the Pandavas were victorious in the epic war, Yuddhishtra, the eldest brother, was deeply saddened by the death of so many relatives. In his middle age (after all, his nephews are sexually active), Yuddhishtra announces his intention of retiring to the forest instead of ascending the throne of Hastinapur. He extols the virtues of *vanaprastha*—compassion toward all, control of body and mind, lack of envy, non-violence and truth. Abandoning the kingdom and all its satisfactions, Yuddhishtra would lead the ascetic's life in the forest to free himself of the depression gripping him: 'I will neither grieve for anyone nor feel joy. I will regard praise and blame alike. Renouncing hope and affection, I will become free and not gather material possessions. . . . I will neither laugh at a person nor disparage anyone. I will always present a cheerful face and will control my senses. I will travel down any road and not ask for directions. I will have no wish to go to any specific place or in any particular direction. There will be no purpose to my comings and goings. I will neither look forward nor glance backwards' (*Mahabharata* [Shantiparva], n.d.; 9: 14–19).

Yuddhishtra's brothers, spokesmen for the other side which espouses an increased involvement in life and affairs, try to convert him to their point of view. Arjuna extolls the merit of having wealth since it makes other ends of life—virtue, sensual pleasure and final liberation—possible. He sees the proposed retirement as an admission of defeat. It is only someone who cannot look after his sons and grandsons, who cannot satisfy the demands of gods, sages and the ancestors, who can be content in the forest.

Another brother, Nakula, stresses the heavy responsibility resting on the shoulders of the middle-aged householder for the 'maintenance of the world' since all beings depend upon him for their protection, sustenance and development. Nakula is not against withdrawal but does not believe that one needs to take the radical step of retiring into the forest; an inner emigration is enough. Renunciation should be of things that ensnare the mind, not of one's home.

Draupadi, the common wife of the five brothers, seeks to persuade her eldest husband that retirement to the forest is only appropriate for brahmins and not barons. Withdrawal from the world, she avers, is for cowards and the impotent who are unable to enjoy its pleasures. Relativizing the traditional ideals of middle age as depending upon the person's station in life, she believes that universal compassion, the taking of alms, studying and asceticism, are virtues of a brahmin not of a king. The highest duty of the king is to wield the rod in punishment of evil doers, protect the good, and never retreat in battlefield. You have not obtained this kingdom by listening to readings from holy books, she tells

Yuddhishtra. The kingdom has not been gifted to you, nor did you get it by convincing others through arguments or through religious rituals and sacrifices. You have obtained it through the force of arms and it behoves you now to enjoy the fruits of your victory.

Yuddhishtra's middle-age crisis, initiated by the carnage of the epic war, persists: 'This earthly kingdom and these various objects of enjoyment do not please my mind today. Sorrow surrounds me from all sides.' After long 'sessions' with some sage-therapists and even with Lord Krishna himself, Yuddhishtra finally comes out of the crisis, regaining his mental equilibrium, with a wider perspective on human life and effort. He understands, for instance, the existential loneliness of a human being: 'Just as a traveller acquires companions on his journey, each one of us has the temporary company of brothers and relatives, wife and children' (28:39). He understands that there is no Divine Giver who can restore to a person what has been lost. He learns the overwhelming role Time plays in human affairs:

Even an intelligent and learned man cannot fulfill his desires if the time is not ripe whereas an ignorant fool gets what he wants if the proper time has come. Time makes the wind blow with the force of gale, time makes the clouds give rain. Time makes the lotus flower and time makes the trees grow strong. Night becomes dark or light through time and it is time which gives the moon its fullness. If the time has not come, trees do not bear flowers or fruits. The current of a river does not become fierce if its time has not come. Birds and snakes and deer and elephants do not come into heat if their time has not come. If the time has not come, women do not conceive. If the time is not ripe, a child is neither born nor dies nor does it pick up speech. Without its proper time, youth does not come and the sown seeds do not sprout (25: 8–11).

Yuddhishtra realizes that sorrow and happiness follow each other and one does not always suffer sorrow or enjoy happiness. Further, 'Happiness and misery, prosperity and adversity, gain and loss, death and life, in their turn wait upon all creatures. For this reason, the wise man of tranquil soul should neither be elated by joy nor crushed by sorrow' (25:31).

The middle-age crisis of renunciation versus involvement is, then, positively resolved through the acquisition of a specific (to use an Eriksonian expression) 'virtue'—*equanimity*. Ideally, the Indian tradition seems to say, the contribution of middle age to human development is a sense of equanimity which is neither a resignation from life nor a withdrawal from human effort and struggle but which provides a person with a wider psychological context for his actions. Equanimity implies the acceptance of the transitoriness of all relationships and emotional states. It includes an awareness that human strivings are insufficient to reach desired goals unless the 'surround', too, is ripe for the success of these efforts. In more psychological language, middle-aged equanimity involves a final renunciation of infantile omnipotence and grandiosity and the Faustian fantasies of youth.

Besides the crisis of involvement versus renunciation and its ideal resolution in equanimity, the second theme which strikes me in Sanskrit texts has to do with middle-aged sexuality. More precisely, the crisis of renunciation versus involvement has the sexuality of this stage of life as one of its central issues. Perhaps the oldest mention of this theme occurs in the *Rigveda* (2500 BC) where Lopamudra who has been waiting for a long time for her ascetic husband to sire a child, says: 'For many autumns past I have toiled, night and day, and each dawn has brought old age closer, age that distorts the glory of bodies. Virile men should go to their wives' (p. 250). The sexual *Torschlusspanik* ('panic before the closing of the door') which is hinted at in Lopamudra's speech makes the middle-aged man especially vulnerable, at least as far as the texts are concerned. Sanskrit literature is replete with middle-aged men's sexual infatuation with young women and the tragic consequences of such autumn–spring unions. In the *Ramayana*, Dasharatha must banish his beloved eldest son Rama to the forest because of the rash promise he has made to Kaikeyi, his fourth and youngest wife with whom he is completely besotted.

In the *Mahabharata*, the king Santanu, Bhishma's father, becomes infatuated with a fisher girl. He goes to the girl's father to ask her hand. The fisherman agrees to the match on the condition that the son born to his daughter inherit the kingdom. Santanu cannot give his consent to this condition. He returns to his palace where he sinks into a depression born of a middle-aged man's unfulfilled passion for a young girl. Bhishma, on coming to know the reason for his father's grief, goes to the fisherman. Bhishma promises both renunciation of the kingdom and of sexual life that could result in a progeny threatening the rights of the sons born to the fisher girl. He then brings the girl to the capital of Santanu's kingdom and hands her over to a grateful father.

From the viewpoint of an outsider, especially an unsympathetic youthful observer, Dasharatha and Santanu cut faintly ridiculous figures. Sanskrit poets, on the other hand, give expression to the personal, subjective side of the middle-aged man's conflict between the ideal of renunciation and the (perhaps inappropriate) demands of his sexual nature. Bharatrihari who, legend has it, continually vacillated between renunciation and sensual indulgence, finding them equally attractive and equally deficient, is a privileged witness of the middle-aged man's difficulties with the 'letting go' of sexual life.

> Cut off all envy, examine the matter,
> tell us decisively, you noble men,
> which we ought to attend upon:
> the sloping side of wilderness mountains
> or the buttocks of women abounding in passion?

and:

> Why all these words and empty prattle?
> Only two worlds are worth a man's devotion:
> The youth of beautiful women wearied by heavy breasts
> and full of fresh wine's excitement,
> or the forest. (p. 61)

Bharatrihari's poems are not the romantic lyrics of a young man or youth's passionate celebration of a woman's beauty. They combine a middle-aged man's clarity of vision in matters of sexual passion together with resentment at his helplessness in the face of such a desire which blurs clarity even as it sharpens it.

> Surely the moon does not rise in her face,
> or a pair of lotuses rest in her eyes,
> or gold compose her body's flesh.
> Yet, duped by poets' hyperbole, even a sage,
> a pondering man, worships the body of a woman—
> a mere concoction of skin and flesh and bones. (p. 68)

The seventh-century poet Mayura is even more stark in depicting the dilemmas of middle-aged sexuality. According to the legend, he wrote his *Mayurastaka* out of his passion for his own daughter—in any case, out of a sexual infatuation which cut across generational boundaries—and was cursed with leprosy as a result. Even in the formalized conventions of Sanskrit poetry, Mayura's sexual vulnerability is palpable.

> Before your father was a youth I was a young man, yet I
> went into the forest when I had seen you, to follow
> and find the coupling place of tigers. His feet
> about the gilded one and his rod flushing out crimson
> were as nothing to my youth,

who am an old man and a King's poet . . .
Rearing the green flame of his tail, the peacock casts the hen beneath him in
the dust of the King's walk. He covers her, and we can hardly see her. She cries
and he cries; and the copper moons in the green bonfire of his tail die down;
and I am an old man. (pp. 108–9)

Besides the desperation of a self-conscious sexuality which the poet
would both keep and let go, Mayura also expresses self-disgust at the hold
his sexuality has on him.

Old maker of careful stanzas as I am, I am also as the fishmonger's ass and smell
to you in riot. He is insensate and does not care though the Royal retinue be
passing. He climbs and is not otherwise contented. And he brays aloud. (p. 110)

The poets, then, take us to the heart of the dilemma of the middle-
aged man as it is represented in ancient Indian literature. Whereas the
Dharmashastras only tell us about the 'oughts' of conduct in the third
quarter of life and the epics of the difficulties that lie in the path of a desired equanimity, the poets isolate the chief obstacle to man's quest for
renunciation—the forsaking of sensual life.

The Life and Times of the Middle Aged Today

In 1980, demographers tell us, three-fourths of the middle aged in
India—defined as the 45–59 age group—lived not only with their aging
spouses but with others as well. These 'others' could be old parents or
close family relatives of the parent's generation as well as married sons and
unmarried children of both sexes (Bhende, 1982). This living pattern has
been changing rapidly in the last fifteen years, especially in middle and
upper middle classes of the metropolitan cities. Thus, a 1988 study of
four hundred students from this class in Delhi revealed that over 80 per
cent lived in families of the nuclear type (Gangrade, 1988). Yet, as a
whole, it would be fair to maintain that a majority of the middle aged in
India today spend their lives in family formations larger than the nuclear
family.

The role of the middle aged in the family is somewhat ambiguous. In
a study of the elderly in a semi-rural community in Delhi, the anthropologist Sylvia Vatuk (1983) found that the ancient ideal of *vanaprastha*
continues to exercise a considerable hold on the Indian imagination.
With the marriage of the first son, which initiates a new reproductive sequence, it is generally expected by the middle-aged couple and by others

in the family and the community that family responsibilities will be handed over to the next generation while the elderly couple increasingly concerns itself with spiritual life and religious contemplation. Although culturally valued and rewarded, this ideal is rarely found in practice. Vatuk observes that this transition in roles seems easier for men who become more and more peripheral to the household's day-to-day activities and shift their interest to the outside world. Most of them are content if they are deferred to by the younger generation, even if the deference is nominal, and as long as they are at least formally consulted in important decisions affecting the family.

For the middle-aged woman, her middle age, which is defined by her assumption of the role of the mother-in-law, the relinquishing of control over the household to the daughter-in-law proves to be a much more difficult task. Proverbs from various parts of the country tell us of the mother-in-law's tenacious clinging to household power and the daughter-in-law's savage wishes in relation to their struggle over it. A Marathi proverb says, '*Sasu gele thik jhale ghardar hati aale*' ('I am glad the mother-in-law is dead, the household is now in my hands'). The proverb has a Hindi counterpart which, translated, says, 'If my mother-in-law died and my father-in-law lived, I (the daughter-in-law) will rule the household.' In Bengali, there is: *Ekla gharer ginni hali bujhi ma; Nishwaske bishwas ki—nadche duto pa*. [On the deathbed of the mother-in-law, the daughter-in-law's mother tells her, 'Understand well my daughter, now you alone will rule this household.' The anxious daughter replies, 'It is not enough to trust the failing breath, her legs are still moving.']

The reluctance of the middle-aged woman to give up her power has partly to do with the vicissitudes of the woman's life cycle in traditional India. As I have elaborated elsewhere (Kakar, 1978), as a daughter a woman is a mere sojourner in her parents' home; as a young bride and daughter-in-law she occupies one of the lowest rungs in her new family where obedience and compliance with the wishes of the elder women of the family, especially those of her mother-in-law, are expected as a matter of course. It is only as she becomes a mother, especially the mother of sons, and ages, that power in the family begins to come her way and seniority holds out enormous rewards not just in status but in actual decision-making.

In life, as in Hindi movies, the middle-aged woman's renunciation of familial power, symbolized by handing over the keys to the household's store of food supplies and linen, occurs after many years of friction, shifting alliances, and—at least in Hindi movies—pleas by various members of the younger generation, '*Maji, ab to aap puja path kariye*' ('Mother, you should now engage yourself in prayer and religious rituals'). In the movies, there is often a scene near the end where the struggle between the mother- and daughter-in-law is finally resolved by the older woman's admission of the younger woman's sterling qualities of character and disposition—about which she had expressed grave misgivings in the beginning. She then hands over the bunch of keys to the daughter-in-law in a ceremonial gesture in front of other assembled family members with the words, '*Bahu* (daughter-in-law), from now on the household is in your charge. I am off to Kashi'—Kashi or Benares being the female counterpart of the 'forest' men in ancient India aspired to proceed to for their retirement.

In actual life, even when they gradually withdraw from direct household responsibilities, middle-aged women (and to a lesser extent, men), try to control the behaviour of younger family members by taking over the role of 'keepers of the tradition'. In this role, ideal for the feelings of moral superiority it engenders in the middle aged and the venomous dislike it produces in the young, the dress, deportment and social interactions of the younger generation are closely monitored and measured against traditional standards and, of course, invariably found wanting. An empirical study of two hundred college students in Jaipur, Rajasthan (Sharma and Bhandari, 1971), reveals that aging men and women are seen by the young as conservatives who dislike any change or interference with established ways of doing things. Young women, perhaps because of their greater contact with the elderly at home and also because their deportment is a special object of the older family members' attention, feel this more strongly than the young men.

With the notions of *ruob* ('authoritativeness') towards the young and *adab* ('respectfulness') towards the old, there is little inter-generational familiarity in India (except, of course, in the upper middle class in the metropolitan centres) as it exists say; in the United States. Men and women seek intimacy with their own age cohorts. Whereas with women this intimacy is generally within the extended circle of the family, men spend more and more time with other middle-aged men of their village and caste community, talking of 'serious' matters and abjuring the frivolous pursuits of their youth, such as going to the cinema.

As for the social status of the middle aged and their relationships with the younger generation, the theology of *burhapa* holds that in traditional Indian society, with its extended family system and well defined hierarchies of power and authority, of age-old channels of respect and obedience, and a socialization that extolls the wisdom of age above the energy of youth, older people are automatically the recipients of deference, respect and all the support and care they need in their declining years. The anthropology of aging (Anantharaman, 1979; Vatuk, 1983; Kumar and Suryanarayna, 1989), on the other hand, reveals this as a myth. It supports the view that from a peak at the onset of middle age, power, authority and prestige decline sharply till in true old age only a husk of deference is left without any real respect. This state of affairs is attributed to the break up of the extended family system as a consequence of modernization. Their traditional skills regarded as obsolete and their experience as irrelevant, the aging are seen by their children and by the larger community as economic and social liabilities. With an increase in the geographical and physical mobility among the young, they no longer receive the care and support which they presumably commanded in earlier, happier times.

Representations in Contemporary Hindi Literature

Reflecting its relative inconsequentiality, both demographic and in popular consciousness, the literary representations of middle age are few and far between. A less than thorough but more than cursory search in contemporary Hindi fiction and poetry unearthed only a few short stories where the main protagonist is clearly middle aged. There are also some poems where childhood memories are summoned by a middle-aged mind or where middle-aged eyes look again at the village where one lived as a child.

Here, I shall take up only one story in some detail—'Silver Wedding' by Manohar Shyam Joshi (1990, pp. 23–40), an immensely popular writer who has enjoyed considerable acclaim for scripting some of the most popular television serials of the last decade.

Yashodar Pant, the 'hero' of the story is what Indian intellectuals and the upper classes derisively, and the rest enviously, call a *babu*, a low-ranking government official in the vast bureaucracy of the Indian state. Perhaps in his late forties or early fifties—the exact age is not clear—Yashodar, nearing the end of his undistinguished career, is the head of a small section in the Ministry of Home Affairs. The story opens on the day of his twenty-fifth wedding anniversary which Yashodar, a man of habit who dislikes any change in his routine, treats like any other day as he prepares to go home at the end of the day's work. Rising from his desk exactly at 5.30 p.m. by his old-fashioned watch (which a younger colleague would have him throw away and replace by a new Japanese digital model), he is asked by his colleagues to order tea and sweets in celebration of his 'silver' wedding anniversary. Yashodar refuses since such celebrations are not a part of his tradition and he finds them, in his two favourite English words 'somehow improper'.

For the last few years, Yashodar has been feeling increasingly alienated from his family. His eldest son has a job in an ad agency and is paid a salary which matches that of his father. Yashodar finds such high salaries paid to the young 'somehow improper'. His second son is preparing for his examinations for the civil service, having refused a perfectly fine job offer into the lower rungs of bureaucracy in the previous year. A third son has gone to the United States to study on a scholarship while the grown-up daughter is refusing all marriage proposals and is threatening to go off to the States for further studies. 'Yashodar *babu* is a democrat and would never insist that the children follow his advice to the letter. But it is too much when none of them even consult him and do exactly what they want. Granted that your knowledge is greater than mine, child, but there is no substitute for experience! Whether you agree or disagree with me, just go through the pretence of consulting me once. The children reply, "*Baba*, you are the limit! Why should we ask you about things of which you have no idea?" ' The children show unmistakable signs that they are going to be of little comfort to him in his old age.

Yashodar's wife too has changed a great deal with middle age. She has become independent and increasingly self-willed. He finds his daughter's wearing of jeans and sleeveless tops 'somehow improper' but his wife is vigorous in the daughter's defence. 'I did all that covering of my head with the sari on your say-so, but my daughter will do exactly what the rest of the world does,' she says. The wife often complains that when she came into his extended family as a bride there were many restrictions placed on her behaviour by her mother- and sisters-in-law and that Yashodar never stood up for her. 'I was young but lived the life of an old woman,' she says. 'The children are quite right in not following your old-fashioned ways and neither will I.' 'Why have you become so serious?' she asks. 'You saw two movies a week when you were young, cooked meat on Sundays and sang *ghazals* and film songs.' Yashodar *babu* accepts that he has changed but feels that with the years a certain kind of age-appropriate maturity (*buzurgiat*) is called for in a man. He tells his wife that the way she has started wearing sleeveless blouses in her *burhapa*, favouring high heels and eating outside the kitchen, are all 'somehow improper'. 'Anyway I am not stopping you from doing all this,' he says, 'therefore you should also not object to my way of life.'

One of his ways which his wife and children strongly disapprove of is his recently acquired habit of stopping by the Birla temple in the evening on his way home from office. Here he listens to discourses of holy men and does some mediation himself. '*Baba*, you are not so old that you should visit the temple daily and engage in all this religious fasting and rituals,' his children complain. Actually, Yashodar *babu* is not very religiously inclined. He is only trying to follow the ideals inculcated in him by his mentor, long since dead, who not only got Yashodar his job but also taught him about life and its meaning. One simply must get more involved in religious and spiritual life as one gets older. Like his mentor before him, Yashodar *babu* too goes to the temple every day, spends time in prayer and the study of religious books. When his mind complains of its disinterest in such activities, Yashodar chides it,' You *should* be interested. Along with the illusory attachment to the world, one has to give God some place in one's life. One should now hand over the kingdom to the younger generation and proceed to the forest.' When Yashodar tries to meditate after his morning and evening prayers, he finds his mind drifting towards family problems rather than contemplating the Almighty. Yashodar would like to learn the the right technique of meditation. He consoles himself with the thought that perhaps the proper time for these practices is after his retirement. They are prescribed for the *vanaprastha* stage and Yashodar *babu* feels he will return to his ancestral village for this stage of his life—'far from the madding crowd, you understand!'

When he reaches home, Yashodar finds that his children have arranged a party for the wedding anniversary to which they have invited their friends. There is cake and whisky—both of which he finds 'somehow improper'—and Yashodar escapes to his room on the pretext of saying his prayers. His eyes closed, he carries on an imaginary conversation with his dead mentor who, echoing the understanding arrived at by Yuddhishtra in the *Mahabharata*, says, 'In the beginning and at the end you are all alone. You cannot call anyone in this world your own.' Yashodar wants to ask his mentor what his attitude should be in face of the difficulties his wife and children are causing him. But the mentor seems bent on talking about the loneliness of this stage of life: 'What wife and what children! That is all *maya* (illusion) and this Bhushan (Yashodar's eldest son) who is today jumping all over the place will one day feel as much alone and helpless as you are feeling today.' Yashodar *babu* would like to carry on this imaginary conversation when he is interrupted by his wife. The guests are leaving and the presents must be unwrapped. One of them is a woollen dressing gown from his eldest son. This is for you to wear instead of that torn old sweater when you go to fetch milk in the morning, says the son. Yashodar's eyes moisten. He does not know whether the unshed tears are because his son has not offered to get the morning milk himself or whether he is reminded of his mentor who, too, used to wear a dressing gown on his morning walks.

'Silver Wedding' highlights some of the themes we have encountered earlier in other accounts of middle age, both in ancient Sanskrit texts and contemporary social science studies. First, the middle aged are conservers of traditional values. In the conflict between tradition, represented by Yashodar's dead mentor, and modernity, represented by his children, Yashodar is squarely on the side of the Hindu tradition which views the renunciation of worldly concerns and a turn toward a more inward, spiritual life as the main task of middle age. The task itself is difficult, more so for women than men, more difficult for Yashodar's wife than for him.

Second, in middle age there is a resurgence of memories of one's childhood and youth, of those who have loved and guided us as we look back at our lives in contemplation. There is a satisfaction afforded by the act of recollection itself, rather than some kind of instrumental 'stock-taking' which has been posited as a dominant concern of the 'mid-life crisis' in the West. As Yashodar gradually liberates himself from the constraints imposed by his career, family and active existence in society in general, his ability to relive the past in his imagination increases. Indeed, as Maurice Halbwachs (1992) observes, this greater capacity to redescend into the past may be related to the social function of the elderly as keepers of the society's traditions, as preservers of traces of its past, and in the encouragement society gives them to devote their energies to acts of remembering.

Third, this stage of life reveals the glimmerings of man's existential loneliness and triggers off the anxiety associated with the glimpses of one's ultimate helplessness. The awareness of this loneliness is inherent in the act of withdrawing from the family and the world, a step recom-mended by Hindu tradition. The underlying anxiety of this momentous mental event is only articulated by writers, the keepers of a society's wishes and fears.

The well-known Hindi writer Nirmal Verma (1983; 1988) has made the depressive loneliness of middle age the focus of two stories: *Sookha* ('Drought') and *Subah ki Sair* ('The Morning Walk'). *Sookha* is narrated from the viewpoint of a young woman, in the first days of her new job as a college lecturer, who has been asked to take care of the dreary details of a literary seminar in a provincial town in Rajasthan, which is in the grip of a drought. The star invitee to the seminar is a middle-aged writer from Delhi who has not written anything for a decade. The story is replete with haunting images of the writer's isolation and lack of contact—the 'drought', of course, is an inner condition rather than an outside event. For a fleeting moment, the woman and the writer come together, a moment of human understanding and sympathy which revives the man, an unexpected shower on a parched inner landscape, before the drought descends again.

Subah Ki Sair describes the morning walk of a retired army colonel who lives alone except for an old servant. His wife is dead and his only son—in the youthful dreams and middle-aged nightmares of Indian middle-class parents—lives in the United States. Nihalchand—that is the colonel's name—spends his time eating, sleeping and talking to himself. The highlight of his day is his morning walk which follows exactly the same route every day and has as its last station a well preserved, deserted Mughal monument—rather like the colonel himself—in the middle of the jungle. Here the colonel eats a frugal breakfast packed by his servant, lies down, closes his eyes and lets a reverie with a strong, hallucinatory quality unroll on his inner screen. A young girl of fourteen, a dearly beloved playmate of his teens, shyly approaches the colonel's prone body. She talks to him about their common memories and asks questions about his wife and son. Nihalchand is not sure whether he is awake or asleep and where these voices are coming from. 'Whose voice was it? Or was it only an illusion, a betrayal. This discordant voice, arising from the jungle of old age, an orphaned, burning voice, knocks at the door. You open the door and there is nothing, only an unending vista of emptiness, no one near or far. No love, no attachment, no pain of infatuation—not even pain. Nothing to be seen, neither the face of his wife nor the remembrance of the son, nothing—only I. Who are you, Nihalchand, what are you?' (1983, p. 73).

In contemporary Hindi fiction and poetry, middle age does not constitute—as in some of Western rhetoric—the 'prime' but rather the decline of life. The prevailing mood is not of optimism and renewed confidence at entering the second half of life but of a barely concealed despair. The desired equanimity of Sanskrit texts has given way to depression; the struggles of ancient poets with middle-aged sexuality are replaced in modern writers by a narcissistic absorption in the minutiae of one's life, past and present.

Movies and Middle Age

In the last decade, there has been a sea-change in the sociological composition of the audience for popular Hindi cinema. Earlier, this cinema catered to the entertainment needs of a predominantly middle-class, 'family' audience. Today, the largest section of its viewership is lower middle class, male, urban youth. Of the many changes in form and content of these movies which this shift in audiences has brought about, it is the relatively low visibility of middle-aged characters which is of special interest to us. Movies have become youth-centred to an unprecedented degree. There is little development of any character other than the young protagonists. Reflecting solely a youthful perspective, the middle-aged characters in the movies—parents, uncles and aunts, bosses at work and others in position of authority—are always seen as fulfilling certain functions in relation to the youthful hero and heroine and have no existence or individuality in their own right. However, as compared to the genuinely old, such as grandparents, who are invariably kindly disposed toward the young, the middle aged are more variable in their representation. Generally, the middle aged in popular Hindi cinema are any one of the following:

Supportive of the young. In these roles, the MA (middle aged) character, often a parent, will show empathy for the hero or the heroine, support his or her aspirations even when these are in opposition to the wishes of the rest of the family. If someone outside the family, but in a position of authority, the MA is firm but kind, a dispenser of wise counsel and, often, also of more concrete, material assistance.

Supportive of the social order. Here, the MA person is a representative of a rigid social order and hidebound morality, most often pertaining to what is and is not a desirable marriage for the offspring. He or she is an unfeeling oppressor of the young who seeks to control their joys and desires. Traditional and conservative, the MA is authoritarian and is solely occupied with finding ways to thwart young love.

Laughable. Here the MA person is caricatured as someone whose eccentricities are a result of some kind of age-related deterioration of the mind.

Or, the MA character is laughable because he or she insists on being youthful, i.e. has not reconciled himself or herself to the loss of youth and to a renunciation of sexuality. This kind of inappropriate behaviour on the MA person's part, which makes him or her an object of derision for the young, is also reflected in popular Hindi sayings. *Seeng kata kar bachda banana* ('to become a calf by cutting off one's horns') is used to describe a middle-aged man foolish enough to hanker after youth while its counterpart for a woman is, *Boodhi ghodi lal lagam; aao logo karo salaam* ('The old mare has red reins; come, people, salute her'). The laughter at the MA—their lack of physical prowess and, sexually, in the gap between promise and performance, is without any sympathetic undertones and reverberates with sarcasm. For the young, this derisive laughter represents an aggressive release from the stranglehold the middle aged have over their lives.

Beta ('Son'), is one of the few box office hits in the last couple of years where the middle-aged characters, even if caricatures, are at least drawn with some attention to detail. Raju, the hero of the story loses his mother at birth and from the age of five has been brought up by his step-mother, Lakshmi. Raju adores Lakshmi with the desperate longing of a mother-less boy although she had married his father only to lay her hands on the family's considerable property. The estate, however, had belonged to Raju's mother who had willed it to her only son and stipulated that he could not sell or gift it till after his marriage and then, too, only with the consent of his wife. In being nice to the boy and turning him into a mother-worshipper, Lakshmi has planned to have the estate signed over to her after Raju grows up. She has kept Raju unlettered, making him work with his share-croppers in the fields, so that she and her brother, who lives with them, can embezzle large sums of money from the estate. The sister and brother have also conspired to have Raju's father declared insane. He is kept confined to one room of their sprawling mansion.

Raju falls in love with Saraswati, a girl from another village and marries her. Lakshmi has no objections since she also needs Raju's wife's signature in order to lay her hands on the property. She is confident that she can easily manipulate her rustic and presumably naive daughter-in-law. However, to make certain that the couple does not develop any strong intimate bond which might threaten her supremacy in the household, Lakshmi tells Saraswati to desist from conjugal relations since astrologers have predicted that Raju would die if he became sexually active before the age of twenty-five.

Saraswati soon sees through her wily mother-in-law's games and proves to be more than a match for her. After an unwise open confrontation in which Saraswati tries to enlighten her husband about her mother-in-law's real character where Raju takes the side of his adored mother and hits Saraswati, the young woman becomes more circumspect in her continuing battle with Lakshmi. She succeeds in having her father-in-law freed from his imprisonment, exposes the financial misdeeds of Lakshmi's brother and cleverly manoeuvers a situation where Lakshmi has no option but to hand over the keys to the stores, and the safe, to her daughter-in-law. To seal her victory at this dramatic highpoint of the movie, she reveals that she is pregnant, i.e., about to become the mother (hopefully) of the all-important son. The last resort for the mother-in-law in their deadly struggle is to try and poison Saraswati. 'In this house only one of us can live', Lakshmi declares to her brother. 'She dares to challenge *me*? Does she not realize that I am a female-snake, quite capable of devouring my own young, to say nothing of destroying hers?' Saraswati finds out that the milk her husband brings her has been poisoned by her mother-in-law. Raju, however, refuses to believe in his step-mother's villainy and to prove Lakshmi's innocence, drinks the milk himself. As he hovers between life and death, Lakshmi finally undergoes a change of heart and allows a doctor to save his life. Alluding to the *Ramayana*, she says, 'Even Kaikeyi (Rama's step-mother) had Rama exiled only for fourteen years and here I was prepared to take my Rama's very life. If I had done so, no one would have ever believed in maternal love again.'

The three middle-aged characters in the film—Lakshmi, her brother, and Raju's father—are obviously viewed from the perspective of the young. The two men are really minor characters, relegated to the sidelines. Raju's father—passive, weak and helpless and yet a 'good' man—is perhaps the most peripheral, an accurate reflection of one major view of the father's role in family life with advancing age. (The other has him as a rampaging household tyrant, terrorizing women and children.) Lakshmi's brother is portrayed as a laughable buffoon, whose villainy is quite ineffectual and depends on the support of his sister for its success.

The central middle-aged character in the movie is undoubtedly Lakshmi. Cold, scheming, and utterly ruthless, Lakshmi is the witch-like mother-in-law of popular Hindu culture. Whereas between the ages of fifteen and thirty, the woman (or rather, her womb) is the object of much praise in sayings and songs for her potential as a mother, the same woman, when she crosses into middle age, i.e. becomes a mother-in-law, is now damned in songs and proverbs as a witch, a snake in female form or a *churel*, a malevolent female ghost. The reason for this transformation, I have discussed earlier, is her supreme authority and command in matters of the household, an authority cordially resented by the daughter-in-law. Besides the discord of this specific role-relationship, it also seems that the entire anger of young women against their socially imposed roles and restrictions becomes channelled in resentment against the mother-in-law. Tamil women ask, 'Will my mother-in-law never die, will my sorrows never end?' while the Marathi saying, 'Mother-in-law died in summer but tears are shed during the monsoon', has its counterparts in other languages. Thus although a middle-aged woman in India enjoys immense authority, there always lies a shadow on her power, a constant undermining of her authority by that part of the culture which mirrors the anger of young women and their wishes to replace her.

This image of the middle-aged woman as a powerful oppressor whose power is under constant sniping is true only for the the mother of adult sons. Middle-aged women without children or those with only daughters are tragic figures and, with the death of their husbands, pitiful, since they have no property rights and must often subsist on the charity of others—an image hauntingly captured by the closely cropped heads of widows bent in prayer or reverie in the pilgrimage centres of Mathura or Benares.

Conclusion

In this essay, I have attempted to elaborate on the Indian (Hindu) ideas of middle age in ancient and contemporary India, noting both the continuities and discontinuities from the past to the present. For the past, I took as my sources such texts as the epics of Ramayana and Mahabharata, the Dharmashastras and Sanskrit poetry. For contemporary India, my sources were popular sayings, Hindi fiction and cinema. My findings can be summarized as below.

Although there is a specific word for middle age in contemporary lexical usage, there is no particular awareness of this period as a separate stage of life. Generally, 'middle age' is considered the first part of old age and is associated with images of decline rather than a 'prime' of life.

There is no particular age explicitly related to the onset of middle age. Both in ancient and modern texts, middle age is heralded by a change in the person's role in family life. Specifically, middle age begins with the marriage of the first child, i.e. the initiation by the next generation of a reproductive sequence of its own.

The chief psychological requirement, the task of this age, as represented in both older and contemporary texts is renunciation of the concerns of family life and of the outside world which had so far dominated adulthood. In ancient poetry and modern fiction, this culturally desired goal of withdrawal triggers off a psychological crisis, especially in men. The Sanskrit poets represent this crisis in terms of the despair associated with a renunciation of sexual life. The old texts see this crisis as one whose successful resolution leads to a specific 'virtue' associated with this stage—a sense of equanimity. In contemporary fictional representations, the crisis is accompanied by a depressive awareness of one's existential loneliness and the frightening images of the helplessness awaiting the person at the end of life.

The culturally desirable goals of renunciation and withdrawal are much more difficult for the middle-aged woman than for the man. Because of certain vicissitudes of the female life cycle in India, the middle-aged woman clings stubbornly to the authority and power in the household which come her way only at this stage of life. An object of resentment for the younger generation, especially her daughters-in-law who constantly try to undermine her power, the middle-aged woman is generally portrayed as an oppressive witch-like character who is secretly scorned by the young.

References

Anantharaman, R. N. (1979), 'Perception of Old Age by Two Generations', *Journal of Psychological Researches,* 23(3), 198–9.

Bharatrihari (1990), *The Hermit and the Love-Thief: The Poems of Bhartarihari,* tr. B. S. Miller, Delhi: Penguin, 1990.

Bhende A. A. (1982), 'Demographic Aspects of Aging in India', in K. G. Desai ed., *Aging in India,* Bombay: Tata Institute of Social Sciences.

Bose, A. B. and Gangrade, K. D. eds (1988), *The Aging in India,* Delhi: Abhinav Publications.

de Souza, A. and Fernandes, W. (1982), *Aging in South Asia,* New Delhi: Indian Social Institute.

Desai, K. G. ed. (1982), *Aging in India,* Bombay: Tata Institute of Social Sciences.

Fernandez, W. (1982), 'Aging in South Asia as Marginalization', in W. Fernandez and A. de Souza eds, *Aging in South Asia,* New Delhi: Indian Social Institute, 1–23.

Gangrade, K. D. (1988), 'Crisis of Values: A Sociological Study of the Old and the

Young', in A. B. Bose and K. D. Gangrade eds, *The Aging in India*, Delhi: Abhinav Publications, 24–35.

Halbwachs, M. (1992), *On Collective Memory*, Chicago: Univ. of Chicago Press.

Joshi, M. S. (1990), 'Silver Wedding', in *Mandir ke Ghat ki Paudhian*, Delhi: Saroj Prakashan, 23–40.

Kakar, S. (1978), *The Inner World: A Psychoanalytic Study of Childhood and Society in India*, Delhi: Oxford Univ. Press.

Kanu, P. et al. (1987), 'Attitude of the Second Generation Toward Aging Problems', in M. L. Sharma ed., *Aging in India*, Delhi: Ajanta.

Kumar, V. and Suryanarayana (1983), 'Problems of the Aged in Rural Sector', in Pati and Jena eds, *Aged in India*.

Mayura (n.d.), 'Amores of Mayura', in E. Power-Mathys ed., *Eastern Love*, vol. IV.

Sharma, K. L. and Bhandari, P. (1971), 'A Study of Students' Stereotypes Toward Aging', *Indian Journal of Gerontology*, 2(1), 20–7.

Sharma, M. L. ed. (1987), *Aging in India*, Delhi: Ajanta.

Vatuk, S. (1983), 'The Family Life of Older People in a Changing Society: India', in J. Soklovsky ed., *Aged in the Third World*: Part II, Williamsburg, Va.: College of William and Mary.

Verma, N. (1983), 'Subah ki Sair', in *Kavve aur Kala Pani*, Delhi: Rajkamal Prakashan, 65–80.

——— (1988), 'Sookha', in *Hansa*, April, 71–86.

9

Rumours and Religious Riots

On 27 February 2002, the Sabarmati Express was allegedly attacked by a Muslim mob at the railway station of Godhra, a small town near Ahmedabad in the state of Gujarat. The train was carrying activists of the Vishva Hindu Parishad (VHP), the religious arm of a resurgent Hindu nationalism, on their way back from Ayodhya, the legendary birthplace of lord Rama, where the VHP was planning to construct a highly contentious temple.

In the attack on the train, around sixty Hindus, mostly men but also some women and children, were burnt alive when their coach was set on fire by the mob. Two days after the gory incident, riots between Hindus and Muslims broke out in many parts of Gujarat, especially in the central districts of the state where both Godhra and Ahmedabad are located. The riots lasted for over a month and claimed more than two thousand lives, mostly of Muslims.

The city of Ahmedabad—the commercial, cultural, and political capital of Gujarat (Gandhinagar, the actual state capital, is more or less a suburb of Ahmedabad)—with a population of more than five million was the worst affected by the riots. Ahmedabad has a tradition of Hindu–Muslim violence going back more than three decades. Indeed, isolated incidents of violence continued to be reported more than six months after the high tide of murder, arson, and looting had subsided.

In September 2002, I collected the rumors that had circulated during the riot from the poorer localities of Ahmedabad—both Hindu and Muslim—where the two communities live in close proximity to each other and which had borne the brunt of violence. A Hindu informant remembered the reception of rumours thus: 'Every day, night or day, many rumours

First published in G.A. Fine, V. Campion-Vincent, and C. Heath (eds), *Rumor Mills: The Social Impact of Rumor and Legend*, New York: Aldine, 2005. A condensed version was published in S. Kakar and K. Kakar, *The Indians: Portrait of a People*, Delhi: Penguin-Viking, 2006.

reached us. They tormented all of us. People couldn't sleep at night. For three months, the rumours deprived us of sleep. They had a very strong effect on women and children; women used to weep after hearing a new rumour and couldn't carry out their household tasks. Men used to stand at crossroads, meet people from outside their locality, and ask about what was happening in other areas. They would then tell others.'

I have been following the role of rumours in religious riots for some time now: the 1947 riots at the partition of the country into the states of India and Pakistan, the 1969 riot in Ahmedabad, and, somewhat more systematically, the Hyderabad riot in 1990. In an earlier study, I described some of my own childhood memories of the rumours that circulated in the north Indian town of Rohtak during the partition (Kakar, 1996). Rumours, lending words and images, however horrific, to the imminent threat of deathly violence against the self and one's community, give rise to complex emotions, not only the feelings of dread and danger but also of exhilaration at the transcendence of individual boundaries and the feelings of closeness and belonging to an entity beyond one's self:

Deriving from the paranoid potential which lies buried in all of us, they [the rumors] were the conversational food which helped in the growth of a collective Hindu body. They sharpened our awareness of our own kind and many, who though they lived in the same bazaar were relative strangers earlier, became brothers overnight. They made misers discover a forgotten generosity as they offered to share food with those who had none; neighbors who had little use for each other now enquired daily about each other's well being. There is little doubt that rumors are the fuel and riots the fire in which a heightened sense of community is also forged. (ibid.: 35)

In this essay, I focus on the content of the rumours that circulated during religious riots in India in Ahmedabad or, more specifically, in the riot-hit areas of the city before making some general remarks on the psychoanalytic 'theory' of rumours.

The Content of Rumours

Of the fifty to sixty rumours I collected from the Hindu and Muslim areas, the ten mentioned most frequently were:

Rumours Circulating in the Hindu Areas

- Large amounts of arms and ammunition have been sent to the Muslims from Pakistan.
- Don't buy anything from the bakery. It will be poisoned.

- The milk has been poisoned. Poison has been injected in the milk pouches.
- Terrorists have infiltrated from across the Kutch border (with Pakistan) and have spread all over Gujarat.
- Don't travel by train. Muslim bands are killing everyone.
- The attack will come at night. Don't go to sleep. Be prepared.
- They kidnap children and train them to be terrorists.
- They are saying castrate all the infidels so that the whole race dies out.
- Don't let girls go out of the house. They kidnap them and do 'bad things' with them.
- Don't go to the central part of the city. There is no protection there.

Rumours Circulating in Muslim Areas

- VHP has announced that you have burnt sixty; we will burn six hundred.
- Islam is in mortal danger. Be prepared.
- Don't let children go out. They kidnap them.
- They are breaking our mosques.
- They are doing bad things with our young women.
- Don't buy milk. It has been poisoned.
- The VHP is giving out weapons on ration cards.
- Don't travel by bus or train. Anything can happen.
- Now they will try to convert us to Hinduism. Be vigilant.
- They force Muslims to say the name of Rama. They kill you if you refuse.

We see that almost half of the rumours are common to both Hindus and Muslims. Of these, except for changes in technology—milk in pouches instead of being delivered by vendors, bakeries instead of grocery shops—some rumours seem to be perennial. In 1990 in Hyderabad, and in Ahmedabad in 1969, I heard essentially the same rumours I had heard as a child in Rohtak. Thus we heard (and in Rohtak believed) that milk vendors had been bribed by the Muslims to poison the milk. Four children were said to be lying unconscious and two dogs had died (in Ahmedabad in 2002, it was a cat) after having drunk the poisoned milk. Many claimed to have personally seen the dogs in the throes of death. Women had hurried to empty out the pails of milk; sticky patches of white soon spread to plaster the cobbled stones of the streets. We heard that Muslims had broken into grocery shops in the night and mixed powdered glass with the salt. A police van was said to be driving around the town, warning people not to buy salt.

I would call the perennial rumours about poisoned food, food that kills instead of nourishing, fundamental rumours: fundamental in the sense that they attack what Erik Erikson (1950) called our sense of 'basic trust', received in our earliest experiences with an empathic mother that lets us experience 'inside' and 'outside' as an interrelated goodness. Poisoned milk makes the secure maternal presence we carry inside us recede. It breaches the individual's 'background of safety', releasing our paranoid potential and its accompanying persecutory anxiety. The persecution anxiety is further heightened by another rumour common to both groups, which attributes danger to hitherto safe activity in common public spaces, such as travel by train and bus.

The second category of rumours that, too, can be described as another perennial favourite, has to do with sexual violence. In our particular case, this category is represented in both groups by the rumour about the rape of the community's women and, additionally, in the Hindu community by the threat of castration of its men. In undermining our familiar controls over mental life, a riot is often experienced as a midwife for unfamiliar, disturbing fantasies and complex emotions. The overcharged atmosphere of violence breathed day in and day out by a person lifts the lid on the cauldron of instinctual drives as civilized sensibility threatens to collapse before the press of instinctuality in both its sexual and violent aspects. Rumours of sexual violence during a riot, and the mixture of horror and relish with which they are recounted, also release the more shameful excitement that bespeaks instinctual desire in its rawer form. Besides expressing moral outrage, rape rumours may well also be used by the men as an unwanted but wished for vicarious satisfaction of their sadistic impulses.

Besides the commonality of some rumours to both communities, there are others that are group-specific and betray the distinct and long-standing fears of each community that rise up to the surface during a riot.

In case of Muslims, these rumours relate to a perceived threat to their religious identity: 'Islam is in danger', 'They are breaking our mosques', 'Now they will try to convert us to Hinduism. Be vigilant', 'They force Muslims to say the name of Rama. They kill you if you refuse' These rumours play into a long-standing fear of Indian Muslims of being swamped by a preponderant and numerous Hindu host. For instance, to protect themselves from possession by malignant spirits, of which minor Hindu divinities—the *devis* and *devatas*—are the most dangerous, Muslims all over the subcontinent are enjoined to be pious and constantly proclaim their faith (Kakar 1982; Ewing 1997). Such calls to the battle stations of faith reflect the primary fear of Indian Muslims of somehow lapsing from the faith and becoming reabsorbed by the insidious Hindu society surrounding them.

Other rumours, specific to the Muslim community although not among the most frequently mentioned, relate to the role of the police. 'Muslims are being arrested and taken away by the police', 'The police are beating any Muslim found on the streets', 'The police are taking away Muslims in trucks and dumping them in Hindu areas where they are killed' are some of the rumours on the partisan role of the predominantly Hindu police. Indeed, in many towns and cities of north India, such as Meerut, confrontations between the police and the Muslims have led to violent explosions.

The community-specific Hindu fear is encapsulated by the rumours: 'Large amounts of arms and ammunitions have been sent to the Muslims from Pakistan' and 'Terrorists have infiltrated from across the Kutch border (with Pakistan) and have spread all over Gujarat'. The mention of 'terrorists' makes these rumours the contemporary version of the rumour I had heard during the 1969 Ahmedabad riot of armed Pakistani agents seen parachuting into the city at night.

Here, by linking it with an armed and dangerous enemy, the Muslim minority becomes a psychological threat that is otherwise not justified by its numbers. The rumours reflect and revive the Hindu nationalist's deep-seated distrust of Muslim loyalty to the Indian state and a doubt regarding Muslim patriotism if the community is faced with a choice between the country of its birth and that of its coreligionists across the border. The rumours conjure up images of a vast Islamic host poised at the country's borders, of medieval Muslim marauders like Mahmud, the sultan of the kingdom of Ghazni, one of the most cruel and rapacious of Muslim invaders, who swept over north India every year like a monsoon of fire and was famed far and wide as the great destroyer of temples and a scourge of the Hindus.

Are the rumours during a religious riot also gendered, in the sense that some rumours are more frequently to be found in the discourse of women than of men? They are not gendered as far as the most common rumours are concerned. However, women, both Hindu and Muslim, seem to show a preference for the more apocalyptic rumours. 'Now there will be war and India will be destroyed', 'They are saying, "Hindus have darkened the sky (with arson), Muslims will dye the earth red (with Hindu blood)"', 'The Lord (*bhagwan*) has taken birth; not a single Muslim will survive now' are three such rumours favoured by Hindu women. 'It is coming to pass as written down in the Koran: universal destruction' is their counterpart among Muslim women.

Women, not unexpectedly, are also partial to rumours pertaining to the safety of their children in the sense that more rumours about the kidnapping of children by the enemy community circulate among women than among men.

To sum up, the most frequently mentioned rumours during the Gujarat violence between Hindus and Muslims have remain relatively unchanged from those of the earlier riots I have been involved with as an observer, going as far back as the partition violence of 1947. The changes, if any, are superficial. Perhaps the cast of villains has been updated: VHP and Bajrang Dal instead of the earlier RSS, Pakistani terrorists instead of Pakistani spies, AK47s instead of rifles, poisoned milk in pouches instead of in pails, but the structure of the rumours has essentially remained the same.

In the rumours common to both Hindus and Muslims, one set of rumours seeks to undermine the individual's sense of 'basic trust', acquired in the earliest phase of life, and thus to set free a paranoid potential and persecutory anxiety on which all rumours will further feed.

Another set of rumours, dealing with the threat of sexual violence, not only further amplifies persecutory fantasies but also weakens the individual's conscious controls of his sadomasochistic impulses.

Besides the sets of rumours subverting individual identity, there is another set of rumours relating to group identity, which magnifies a group's specific and historically derived fear in relation to the 'enemy' group. In Muslims the fear is of reabsorption in Hindu society, while in Hindus it relates to the threat to the freedom of the country and a dreaded revival of medieval Muslim suzerainty.

The Process of Rumours

There is no psychoanalytic theory of rumours. There is, however, a nascent theory of gossip (Rosenbaum and Subrin, 1963; Olnick, 1980), which can be mined to advance a few propositions on the psychological role of rumours in situations of grave danger. Rumour, of course, is closely related to gossip in the sense that it is a communicative activity more characteristic of large groups and organizations and uses unconscious fantasies held in common by members of the larger group, rather than the more intimate smaller social circle in which gossip typically circulates. In our particular context, though, rumour is not only a more dignified term for gossip but is also less benign in its content and more dangerous in its consequences.

At the level of the ego processes involved, rumour and gossip appear to be identical. Like gossip, rumour involves the feelings of curiosity, transient identification, and intimacy. The evocation and engagement of the curiosity of the listeners to a piece of gossip or to a rumour start a process in which the purveyor and the 'purveyees' are united in an action that leads to increased feelings of kinship and intimacy. Because of the atmosphere of imminent violence and threat to life and limb of one's loved ones, the pleasure of gratified curiosity produced by a rumour is not as much in the foreground as it is in gossip. What is pivotal here are the strong mutual identifications and feelings of kinship produced by partaking of rumours, what Bordia and DiFonzo (Chapter 5 in this volume) call 'relationship-enhancing'. Furthermore, infinitely more than in gossip, rumours impart an adrenaline-like 'rush of life' to their recipients, making people feel more alive than in normal, everyday life. In strengthening an individual's identity with his or her group, rumour helps in releasing the feelings of exaltation connected with the transcendence of individual boundaries.

Gossip and rumour also differ in the relative importance each accords to envy vis-à-vis anxiety. Envy, which is a sine qua non for gossip (Olnick, 1980) cedes its pre-eminent position to anxiety in case of rumour. In other words, the discharge of hostility and the vicarious pleasure of sexual fantasies that are projected onto the gossipee, and then introjected by the gossipers (Rosenbaum and Subrin, 1963) are less important in rumours than the attempts of the individual and the group to master anxiety in a situation of grave danger. As we saw above, the discharge of aggression is not absent in rumour. Neither is the vicarious enjoyment of sexual impulses, although compared to gossip, the sexual impulses in rumour are primarily of a sadomasochistic kind and thus have a much greater component of aggression. The discharge of aggression and the pleasure of vicarious sexuality are, however, subordinated to the rumour's primary function of mastering anxiety in situations of grave danger, such as a religious riot.

References

Erikson, Erik (1950), *Childhood and Society*, New York: Norton.

Ewing, Katherine P. (1997), *Arguing Sainthood: Modernity, Psychoanalysis and Islam*, Durham, NC: Duke University Press.

Kakar, Sudhir (1982), *Shamans, Mystics and Doctors*, New York: Knopf.

——— (1996), *The Colors of Violence*, Chicago: University of Chicago Press.

Olnick, Stanley L. (1980), 'The Gossiping Psychoanalyst', *International Review of Psycho-Analysis*, 7: 439–45.

Rosenbaum, John M. and Mayer Subrin (1963), 'The Psychology of Gossip', *Journal of the American Psychoanalytic Association*, 11: 817–29.

10

On the Psychology of Islamist Terrorism

Religion and terrorism have a long common history. Some of the words used in English language to characterize a terrorist are either closely connected with religion or are derived from the names of religious groups. A fanatic, for example, derives from *fanum*, the Latin for temple, someone who suffered from temple madness. A zealot refers to a Jewish sect that fought against the Romans in Israel in the first century. Using a primitive form of chemical warfare, they poisoned wells and granaries used by the Romans. The zealots even sabotaged Jerusalem's water supply besides indulging in individual acts of assassination. Which brings us to assassin, literally 'hashish-eater', a radical Muslim Shia sect, which fought the Christian crusaders between the 11th and 13th centuries. The assassins looked upon murder as a sacred duty that would hasten the coming of a new millennium. If he would die in the course of committing his act, the assassin was promised an entry into a glorious heaven. His was an ethos of self-sacrifice and martyrdom that is still present in Islamist terror movements today.

Until the advent of nationalism, anarchism, and Marxism, religion provided the only justification for terror. Even today, the violence committed by relatively more secular terror groups such as the Irish Republican Army, the Sri Lankan LTTE, the Basque ETA, the Shining Path in Peru, and the now defunct Bader-Meinhof group in Germany and the Red Brigade in Italy pales in comparison with the horrors that become possible when the terrorists are religious fundamentalists or when a nationalist-separatist terrorist movement also becomes imbued with religious fervour. The London blasts are the most recent but I am sure that none of us have

First published in German in *Die Zeit*; the English version appeared in *The Asian Age*.

forgotten the horrors of Madrid train bombings or the school massacre in Chechnya. Holy terrorists, as we shall see later, although sharing some of the terrorist psychology with their secular counterparts, have nevertheless completely different value systems, concepts of morality, and ways in which they justify and legitimize their terrorist acts.

A terrorist does not enter the world as a finished terrorist. He, and increasingly she, arises from a large minority of Muslims all over the world who have made the fundamentalist message of a radical Islam their own. Let us listen closely to this message because I believe it is generally misunderstood in the West. This message, which I have described in detail in my book *The Colours of Violence* (1996), is preached by fundamentalist preachers in some mosques and traditional Koranic schools, the madrasas. It generally begins with a lament for the lost glories of Islam, as the preacher compares the sorry plight of Muslims today with their earlier exalted status. Look at the sorry fate of Iraq, a land made sacred by the blood of the Prophet's grandsons, says one mullah. At one time Sultan Saladin commanding a force of thirteen thousand in the battle for Jerusalem faced Richard's army of seven hundred thousand and killed three hundred Christians on a single day. Once in the battle for Mecca, the Prophet with a ragtag force of three hundred and thirteen, including women and children, defeated the one thousand warriors of Abu Jahl, many of them on horseback. Today, with all the oil, dollars, and weapons in the world, Muslims are slaves to Western Christian powers even in lands where they are supposed to be the rulers.

After listing the symptoms of Muslim distress, the mullahs proceed to diagnose the disease. The bad condition of Muslims, they aver, is due to a glaring internal fault: the weakening or loss of religious faith. Muslims have lost everything—political authority, respect, the wealth of both faith (*deen*) and the world (*duniya*)—because they did not keep their pact with Mohammed. At one time Allah gave Muslims the kingdom of the world only in order to test them whether they would continue to remain His slaves. It was their religious zeal which made a small group of Muslims succeed against overwhelming odds. The Arabs, in spite of their wealth, a territory 650 times larger, and a population fifty times greater, are humiliated by Israel because they are only fighting for land even if it is there own land. They are not fighting for Islam. They are not fighting for the Prophet. Sultan Saladin fought for Islam, and won Palestine. On the eve of his battle with Richard, he said to his soldiers, 'Paradise is near, Egypt is far'.

After listing the symptoms and making the diagnosis, the fundamentalist doctor proceeds to the third step of his clinical investigation: pathogenesis.

The disease is caused by the process of modernity and globalization, which the Muslim body has not resisted. There is no difference today between the home of a Muslim and that of a Jew, Hindu, or Christian. The remedy, then, is a return to the Shariat and the fundamentals of the faith as contained in the Koran.

This constant depiction of a despised present as something dark and degenerate, whereas the past and a hoped-for future are shining and glorious, is one of the ideological underpinnings of the terrorist's readiness to embrace death in carrying out his mission. As Erich Hoffer in his classic *The True Believer* (2002) put it, 'To lose one's life is but to lose the present and, clearly, to lose a defiled, worthless present is not to lose much.'

Psychologically, then, fundamentalism is a theory of suffering and cure which has replaced the economic, political, social accounts of contemporary Muslim suffering in some parts of the world with a religious account, complete in itself, on the symptoms, causes, origins, and remedy for the suffering. Illness to the outsider, fundamentalism is a cure for the insider. For many Muslims with an inchoate sense of oppression and the looming shadow of a menacing future, with fractured self-esteem in wake of historical change, fundamentalism is an attempt, however flawed, to revive the sacred in social and cultural life. It is an attempt to give politics a spiritual dimension, and to recover in their religious truths a bulwark against collective identity fragmentation.

One of the prime elements of the cure is effort or jihad—the root word of jihad in Arabic means utmost effort. Jihad is the effort or struggle against the obstacles that prevent a believer from living the perfect Islamic life, of living life in the faith. Jihad, then, is both a peaceful struggle against the temptations of one's own lower nature and an armed struggle against the outer forces of unbelief, *kufr*, that prevent one living in belief.

The motor of the jihad, then, is not in its lack of values. Only that these values are different from the ones that govern modern sensibility. In a globalizing world that calls for making choices in everyday life, fundamentalism would have nothing to do with the desirability of increasing human choice. In his essay 'The Psychological Sources of Islamic Terrorism', Michael Mazarr (2004) puts it succinctly when he says that in a modern world that asks for reasons, fundamentalism is a beleaguered tradition that defends tradition in a traditional way, by reference to a revealed truth beyond human enquiry. We can go badly wrong if we see jihadis as President Bush does, as thugs, as people who hate freedom clashing with freedom-loving Americans. His statement reminds me of one attributed to Dostoevsky: 'While nothing is easier than to denounce the evildoer, nothing is more difficult than to understand him.' It is not the hate of Western democracy but the fear of contagion by Western culture's *impurities* that fuel jihad. The jihad's dread is not of political freedom but of moral pollution. This becomes crystal clear if we look at the essential charter of the jihad movement, its *Mein Kampf.* This is a text called *Milestones.* It was penned by Sayyid Qutb, the founder of the militant Muslim Brotherhood in Egypt. Sayyid Qutb wrote down his thoughts after his travels in the USA between 1948 and 1950, shortly before Nasser executed him in 1966. In his essay 'My Holy Warrior', Jonathan Raban (2002) tells us that according to Qutb, drinking, fornication, shopping, and vulgar entertainment were the chief pursuits of a spiritually and morally bankrupt society sunk in *jahaliya* (remember the Prophet's defeat of Abu Jahal?), the condition of ignorance, barbarism, from which the Arabs were rescued by the gift of Koran. The twentieth century, dominated by Western cultural forms, is a new jahaliya and the great project of a revived Islam is to restore the rule of Allah globally, by force of arms if necessary. Ironically, Sayyid Qutb echoes President Bush even as he reverses the American president's classification of who are the lovers and haters of freedom. '. . . this religion [Islam] is really a universal declaration of the freedom of man from servitude to other and from servitude to his own desires. It is a declaration that sovereignty belongs to God alone and that he is the Lord of all the worlds.' Wherever Allah's sovereignty is not acknowledged is a place ripe for spurning, if not burning. 'There is only one place on earth which can be called the house of peace, and it is that place where an Islamic state is established and the Shariah [Koranic law] is the authority and God's laws are observed . . . The rest of the world is the place of war.'

Let me say here that although the terrorist arises from the fundamentalist, most fundamentalists are not terrorists. Although many may sympathize with the outer, armed jihad of the terrorist, their own energies are concentrated on the inner jihad of leading the pious life of a believer. The fundamentalist, too, feels the humiliation of the nation of Islam. But unlike the terrorist, his anger is directed inward in a collective self-recrimination. His feelings are more of a victim, of helplessness, and, in the elite, sadness in mourning the lost glories of Islamic civilization.

The reaction to feelings of humiliation takes a profound and fatefully different turn in the terrorist—the *mujahdeen* (holy warrior) or jihadi, as he would call himself. His need for revenge, for righting a wrong, for undoing a hurt by whatever means is a deeply anchored, unrelenting compulsion in the pursuit of these aims. His vengeful attitude, gives him no rest, kills all feelings of empathy for those who are perceived to belong to the enemy—whether women or children—that is equated with Satan. The jihadi, then, is psychologically organized around a cold rage and revenge becomes the purpose of his being. This is as terrifying as it is tragic. Tragic, because he sees in terrorism, in what appear as totally evil acts, an arena for heroism and idealism. He becomes even more frightening in view of the fact that he is neither mad nor crazed with drugs as many would like to believe. His reasoning capacity, while totally under the domination and in the service of the overriding emotion, a total commitment to hatred, is often not only intact but even sharpened and more focused.

There are many factors that contribute to this difference between the psychologies of the fundamentalist and the jihadi. Let me begin with the role the religious group plays on the stage of their inner worlds. All of us are members of many groups—family, profession, co-workers, region, nation, religion. Each of these groups influences our beliefs, attitudes, and behaviour at different times and in different proportions. In case of a threat, challenge, or even insult to one of these groups, the particular identity associated with this group comes to the forefront in our consciousness. The attitude and behaviour associated with this identity recedes again once the crisis is over. In case of the jihadi, there is a permanent switchover to the religious group identity and a rejection of the salience of all other groups. Radical Islam becomes the dominant or even the sole mode of experiencing his group identity. The jihadi is not a person who wears his religious group identity lightly; for him it is an armour that is rarely, if ever, taken off. His behaviour, whether in time of peace or heightened conflict, is dictated by his particular puritan, fundamentalist religious commitment that enjoins kindness and compassion to those he considers his own and an implacable hatred toward those who are outside the fold.

What are the differences between the religious and the secular terrorist? As compared to the secular terrorist whose aims are limited to achievement of circumscribed political objectives, the goal of the religious terrorist is more encompassing. His is a Holy War, which can only end when total victory over the world of kufr has been achieved

The religious inspiration for terrorist acts takes away any guilt associated with the taking of innocent lives. The religious inspiration, with its portrayal of conflict as being between the forces of God and Satan, good and evil, enables the religious terrorist to contemplate far more deadly operations than the secular terrorist and a larger, much less circumscribed category of enemy for attack. His goals, sacred by definition, are exempt from all forms of human enquiry. He sees his violence as that of a soldier in defense of his faith, a higher calling than that of a soldier merely defending his country. His violence, which is sacred in that it is absolute, beyond appeal, unanswerable to human reason, is a violence that exalts rather than diminishes him.

The exaltation is especially true of the 'suicide-bomber'. He is not like the 'normal' suicidal person who acts out of despair and feelings of utter helplessness. The suicide-bomber would lose the religious validation, even elevation, of his action if he ever did so. For according to his theology, a suicide who kills himself for personal reasons is committing a heinous and blasphemous action. In 'Mishandling Suicide Terrorism', the anthropologist Scott Atran quotes Sheikh al-Kardawi, the most important Sunni religious authority for martyr actions: '. . . he who commits martyrdom sacrifices himself for the sake of his religion and nation [nation in the sense of nation of faith, of Islam].' In contrast to the hopelessness of the ordinary suicide, '. . . the Mujhaid is full of hope. They are youth at the peak of their blooming who at a certain moment decide to turn their bodies into body parts . . . flowers.' (Atran, 2002, p. 76)

One reason for the terrorist's donning of the religious armor is the demographic background of most terrorists. When Colin Powell (2002) tells the World Economic Forum that 'terrorism really flourishes in areas of poverty, despair and hopelessness', he is mistaken. Atran (2004) analyses the relevant studies to show terrorists to be more educated and economically better off than the population to which they belong. A majority of Palestinian suicide bombers have a college education (as compared to 15 per cent of the population of the same age group) and less than 15 per cent come from poor families. The interrogation of Saudi Arabian detainees concludes that a surprising number have graduate degrees and come from high status families. The Singapore Parliamentary report on prisoners from Jemaah Islamiya, an ally of Al-Qaeda, similarly reaches the conclusion that these men were not ignorant, destitute, or disenfranchised but held normal, respectable jobs. (Atran, 2004, p. 20).

In his book *Islam in a Globalizing World* (2003), Thomas Simons, a long-time, sympathetic student of the Islamic world and a former US ambassador to Pakistan, compares the terrorists of revolutionary Russia with those of the Islamic world today. 'The young of both times and places—the Russian world after 1870 and the Arab world around 1970—were scarred by the frustration of always living second-rate lives in relation to those at the cutting edge of globalization . . . This reality is painful, and the pain often is felt most keenly not by the poorest, but by those who have progressed a little and are frustrated in their aspirations to go further.'

These educated and materially better-off Muslims are more likely to be aware of their history. They resonate more to accounts of past Islamic glory and the present marginal state of most Islamic nations, and are thus more prone to the feelings of collective humiliation. More than their other coreligionists, they are extremely sensitive to Western triumphalist rhetoric on the backwardness of Muslim societies and a crowing about the achievements and superiority of Western civilization. For them, killing of Muslim men in armed clashes or even bombing and missile attacks that kill civilians, are not as bad as a continuing occupation of lands Muslims consider their own. Acts that shame Muslims, such as the events in the Iraqi prison of Abu Gharib, are the worst.

His education and class background also makes the terrorist more sensitive to the oppressive structures of his own society, and of the modern world. His consciousness is thus marked by an inner sense of oppression. He is thus more likely to find tyranny wherever he settles down in the world. Living in a liberal Britain, France or Germany or Spain does not make the potential terrorist more liberal. On the contrary, believing to be surrounded by kufr—unbelief—the budding terrorist lives in exile in a chronic state of persecution and a horror of pollution by the Western world that surrounds him, making his adherence to his radical theology even stronger.

Let me note here that the response to humiliation, which has been advanced as the main motivation of the terrorist, does not mean that there are no other subsidiary motivations that come into play. As Jessica Stern (2003), a terrorism expert at Harvard has observed, terrorism also holds a promise of adventure and glamour that can be attractive to many young males (p. 44). Others may be attracted by the material rewards of terrorism, which pays better than conventional employment in an impoverished country. Also, although feelings of humiliation and its avenging is the main psychological motor of Islamist terror, this motivation is not of equal strength across all Muslim populations. Arab societies, with their much greater sensitivity to the calculus of shame and honour, are more vulnerable to perceived humiliations and injuries to narcissism, the feeling of grandiosity, than other Muslim societies where the honour-shame calculus—the gaining of lost honour by avenging shame—is not quite as pronounced.

References

Atran, S. (2004), 'Mishandling Suicide Terrorism', *Washington Quarterly*, 27(3): 67–90.

—— (2004), 'Soft Power and the Psychology of Suicide Bombing', *Terrorism Monitor*, 2: 11.

Hoffer, E. (2002), *The True Believer*, New York: Perrenial Classics.

Kakar, S. (1996), *The Colours of Violence*, Delhi: Penguin-Viking.

Mazarr, J.M. (2004), 'The Psychological Sources of Islamic Terrorism', *Policy Review*, 126.

Powell, C. (2002), 'World Economic Forum', *New York Times*, 2 February 2002.

Raban, J. (2002), 'My Holy War', *The New Yorker*, 4 February 2002.

Simons, T. (2003), *Islam in a Globalizing World*, Stanford: Stanford University Press.

Stern, J. (2003), *Terrorism in the Name of God*, New York: HarperCollins.

Index